D0897840

Principles of Mental Imagery

Principles of Mental Imagery

Ronald A. Finke

MAY 1991

ELMHURST COLLEGE LIBRARY

A Bradford Book

The MIT Press
Cambridge, Massachusetts
London, England

© 1989 Massachusetts Institute of Technology

All rights reserved. No part of this book may be reproduced in any form by any electronic or mechanical means (including photocopying, recording, or information storage and retrieval) without permission in writing from the publisher.

This book was set in Palatino by DEKR Corporation Inc. and printed and bound by Halliday Lithograph in the United States of America.

Library of Congress Cataloging-in-Publication Data

Finke, Ronald A.
  Principles of mental imagery / Ronald A. Finke.
    p.   cm.
  "A Bradford book."
  Bibliography: p.
  Includes index.
  ISBN 0-262-06122-8
  1. Imagery (Psychology)   I. Title.
BF367.F56   1989
153.3′2—dc19   89-2312
                                                                           CIP

Contents

Acknowledgments

I am indebted to my friends and colleagues, who have contributed in many ways to the ideas developed in this book: Steven Pinker, Jennifer Freyd, Roger Shepard, Howard Kurtzman, Marty Schmidt, Martha Farah, Marcia Johnson, Marvin Levine, and Gary Shyi.

I am also grateful to my teachers, who over the years have led me to this project: Richard Held, Ernest Hilgard, Milton Erickson, Mary Potter, Judith Thomson, and Tom McMahon.

In addition, I would like to thank Mary Anne Huntington for her excellent work in preparing the figures. Portions of the author's research were supported by Grant 5R01MH-3980903 from the National Institute of Mental Health.

Principles of Mental Imagery

Chapter 1

Information Retrieval Using Mental Images

1.1 The Scientific Challenge of Imagery Research

People often wonder why mental images resemble the things they depict. For example, an image of a pizza mentally "looks" something like an actual pizza. An image of a football spinning around mentally "looks" something like the way a spinning football actually does look. Because mental images frequently accompany our waking thoughts and our dreams, they naturally arouse our curiosity about their nature and purpose.

How could one go about doing scientific experiments to discover the actual properties and functions of images? This presents one of the most difficult yet exciting challenges for a research scientist.

One reason the scientific study of mental imagery is so challenging is that imagery is a *subjective* phenomenon. Unlike physical objects, mental images are not directly "observable"; hence, their properties and functions always have to be inferred. You can't simply rely on what people tell you about their images because subjective reports are often inaccurate and unreliable. For example, suppose someone told you that his or her image of an apple was "round, red, and shiny." How would you verify such a claim? At the very least, you would need to have some source of objective evidence that is not based entirely on subjective impressions.

Another reason is that images are notoriously elusive—they can appear one moment and quickly fade the next. Experimental methods are needed that permit one not only to infer the properties of images in an objective, scientific manner but also to reliably elicit the images themselves. The difficulties in doing so often tax the researcher's ingenuity and resourcefulness to the limit, at times making the study of imagery as controversial as it is fascinating.

Searching for these scientific methods is well worth the effort, because many long-standing philosophical issues could be resolved if only we knew more about the nature of imagery. For example, is mental imagery truly different from other, more abstract ways of thinking? What, precisely, do imagery and perception have in common? Do mental images obey the same laws as physical objects? These are empirical questions requiring appropriately designed research studies; they cannot be answered by philosophical debate alone (see Block 1981; Dennett 1978).

There are many practical reasons as well for conducting scientific investigations of mental imagery. For instance, many popular techniques for improving memory are based on visualization. People often claim that imagery plays a role in solving problems and in making creative discoveries. Imagery has long been used in psychotherapy, especially in reducing anxiety. What is it about imagery that makes these applications possible? What other potential applications of imagery might exist? Again, these are challenging questions for researchers.

This book will describe how the study of mental imagery has been transformed into an empirical science as a result of a number of recently invented experimental techniques. The experiments I will discuss are taken mostly from research on visual imagery that I and my colleagues have been conducting over the past ten years. This research has led to the identification of five major principles of imagery: the principle of *implicit encoding*, the principle of *perceptual equivalence*, the principle of *spatial equivalence*, the principle of *transformational equivalence*, and the principle of *structural equivalence*. Taken together, these five principles provide a general description of the fundamental characteristics of mental images. There will be some exceptions to these principles, and they are limited in certain respects, but I will argue that they are essentially correct.

Before considering these principles in detail, I would like to define how the term "mental imagery" will be used throughout this book.

1.2 A Definition of Mental Imagery

"Mental imagery" is defined as *the mental invention or recreation of an experience that in at least some respects resembles the experience of actually perceiving an object or an event, either in conjunction with, or in the absence of, direct sensory stimulation.* This is certainly not the only definition of mental imagery that one could propose, but it is a convenient working definition for the scientific investigations that will be reported here.

This usage of the term "image" is quite different from its use in the visual sciences to refer to the projection of visual scenes on the back of the retina (Marr 1982). It is also different from the use of the term "iconic image" to refer to the short-term retention of visual information in sensory mechanisms (Neisser 1967; see also Sperling 1960). As the experiments in this book will show, mental images are very different from either retinal or iconic images.

1.3 Questions That Elicit Images

I shall begin by taking up a very basic question about mental imagery: Are mental images, in the sense just defined, really any different from other kinds of mental representations, such as verbal descriptions? Because most people claim that they can form mental images, and that their images often "resemble" actual physical objects, the *subjective* reality of mental imagery and its distinctiveness from verbal thinking can hardly be denied. But is there any *objective* evidence that images are distinct from thoughts made up of words or sentences? How could you show this?

1.3.1 Some Simple Demonstrations

One way is to try to show that forming mental images, as opposed to thinking about something in terms of verbal descriptions, is necessary in order to answer certain types of questions. For instance, consider the following questions: What color is the top stripe of the American flag? Did Thomas Jefferson have a beard? Most people say that they have to imagine looking at a mental "picture" of the American flag or Thomas Jefferson's face before they can tell. By examining the way people give answers to such questions, perhaps one could show that mental images really are distinct from verbal descriptions.

There would still be a problem, however, if all you had to rely on was what people *told* you. Even if you found that when people say they are using images, they tend to be more successful in coming up with the correct answers, you would still not convince a skeptic. A person's introspections about what he or she did to answer a question could be completely wrong. *You also need to show that giving the correct response depends on whether or not it is easy to extract the needed information from the image.* This would provide more convincing evidence that mental imagery is distinct from other forms of information retrieval.

1.3.2 Interfering with Mental Images

An ingenious technique for showing that images are distinct from verbal processes was invented by Lee Brooks. In one of his experiments, subjects were told to report whether or not each successive corner of a block letter, such as a capital F, was at the extreme top or bottom, when recalling the letter from memory (Brooks 1968). The subjects were to do this by starting from a particular corner (labeled by an asterisk) and then continuing in the clockwise direction. For example, using the block letter F shown in figure 1.1, the correct sequence of responses would be "yes, yes, yes, no, no, no, no, no, no, yes." As the reader may verify, when doing the task from memory, one is virtually compelled to form and inspect a mental image of the letter.

Brooks also varied the *manner* in which the subjects were to give their responses. In one condition, they were simply to say "yes" or "no" to indicate whether the successive corners of the letter were at the extreme top or bottom. In another, they were to give their responses by pointing to the letters Y and N printed in rows on a response sheet. These rows were staggered so that the subjects would have to visually attend to the letters as they responded. It took them an average of 11.3 seconds to complete the task when they gave their responses verbally, but an average of 28.2 seconds when they gave their responses by pointing. This increase in response time would make sense if the pointing responses, which had to be visually guided, had interfered with maintaining and using an image of the letter. The implication is that *a mental image must be more like a "picture" of something than a verbal description.*

There are, however, other possible explanations for this finding. For example, it might always take longer to respond by pointing to letters that designate words than by saying the words out loud. To rule out this possibility, Brooks included a second task in which subjects first were read a sentence and then had to indicate whether

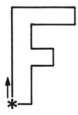

Figure 1.1
Example of a task that demonstrates how mental imagery can be used to retrieve information from memory. Subjects in the experiment had to say whether or not the consecutive corners of a previously seen block letter, such as the one illustrated above, were at the extreme top or bottom, starting from the corner designated by the asterisk. (from Brooks 1968)

or not each successive word in the sentence was a concrete noun. For example, in the sentence "A bird in the hand is not in the bush," the correct sequence of responses would be "no, yes, no, no, yes, no, no, no, no, yes." As in the previous task, the subjects gave their responses either by saying the words "yes" and "no," or by pointing to the letters Y or N on a response sheet. This time, it took them longer to respond verbally (13.8 seconds) than by pointing (9.8 seconds), just the opposite of what had been found in the block letter task. These contrasting results, which are presented in figure 1.2, led Brooks to conclude that the pointing responses interfered more with mental imagery, whereas the verbal responses interfered more with the verbal recall of sentences. The distinction between imagery and verbal processes was thus demonstrated without reliance on introspective reports. (See also Brooks 1967, 1970 for related findings.)

1.3.3 The Symbolic Distance Effect
Other types of questions can also elicit mental images and can be employed to study imagery scientifically. For instance, which is larger, a pineapple or a coconut? Most people claim that they imagine the two objects next to each other, rather than recall descriptions of them, to determine the answer. These mental comparisons are fairly

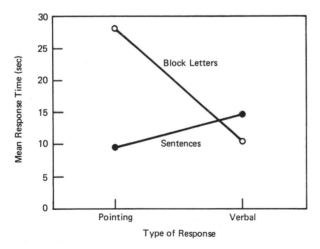

Figure 1.2
Mean response time to complete the block letter task and the corresponding task of identifying consecutive words as nouns in remembered sentences, depending on whether the responses were given verbally or by pointing to printed letters on a visual display. The interaction of the functions suggests that visually guided pointing selectively interferes with mental imagery. (from Brooks 1968)

easy when the objects are very different in size but seem much harder when the objects are similar in size. It is easier to tell from an image that a beaver is larger than a squirrel, for example, than to tell that a beaver is larger than a raccoon. This suggests another method for distinguishing images experimentally from verbal descriptions: *It should take less time to make mental comparisons between things that are increasingly different in size, independent of how one might describe them.*

It turns out that there is a lawful relationship, called the *symbolic distance effect*, between the time it takes to make these comparisons and the relative size of the objects: To a good approximation, the response time is inversely proportional to the relative difference in size. This effect was first reported by Robert Moyer (1973). He presented subjects with pairs of animal names (for instance, "ant" and "bee" or "frog" and "bear"), and their task was to choose the name corresponding to the larger animal. Moyer found that the response time for judging the larger of the two animals increased as the size difference between the animals decreased.

These findings correspond to those that are typically obtained when people judge the larger of two objects while actually looking at the objects (Paivio 1975). Moyer concluded, therefore, that mental images of the animals were being used to make visual comparisons of their size differences, just as if the animals were actually present. Similar findings have also been reported when subjects are specifically told to use imagery to make these comparisons (Holyoak 1977) and when the comparisons involve geometric figures, where the differences in size are completely arbitrary (Moyer and Bayer 1976). The symbolic distance effect is hard to explain if what people do is simply retrieve verbal descriptions of the remembered items, but it is easily understood if they rely on mental imagery to make their judgments.

A subsequent study by Kosslyn, Murphy, Bemesderfer, and Feinstein (1977) provided even stronger evidence that mental images, not verbal descriptions, are responsible for the symbolic distance effect. Subjects began by learning a set of stick figures varying in color and size. The figures were explicitly labeled as "large" or "small," with half of the set in each size category. Two of the figures were then designated by naming their respective colors, and the subjects reported, from memory, which figure was larger. When the figures were taken from the same size category (both were "large" or both "small"), reaction times for identifying the larger figure increased as the size difference between the figures decreased, again producing the symbolic distance effect. However, when the figures were taken from different size categories and the labels were highly overlearned, the symbolic distance effect did not occur (see figure 1.3). In this case, the subjects were able to use the remembered verbal labels to make the correct judgments, and the actual differences in size be-tween the figures did not matter.

1.4 The Implicit Encoding Principle

These findings can all be accounted for by a general principle that specifies the role that imagery plays in retrieving information from memory. This is the *implicit encoding* principle, which has been sug-gested, in a slightly different form, by one of my colleagues, Steven Pinker (see Pinker 1984). It may be stated as follows:

Mental imagery is instrumental in retrieving information about the phys-ical properties of objects, or about physical relationships among objects, that was not explicitly encoded at any previous time.

By saying that information is "implicitly" encoded, I don't mean *subliminally*; that is, without awareness of the stimulus (Erdelyi 1974; Marcel 1983). Rather, I simply mean that the information was not intentionally committed to memory prior to its being retrieved.

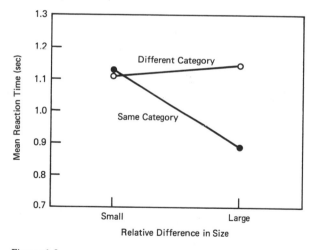

Figure 1.3
Mean reaction time to select, from memory, the larger of two stick figures, depending on their actual differences in size and whether they came from the same size categories. (The figures had each been previously labeled as "small" or "large.") The reaction time functions show that the symbolic distance effect is eliminated when highly overlearned descriptive labels are used to compare the sizes of remembered objects. (from Kosslyn, Murphy, Bemesderfer, and Feinstein 1977)

1.4.1 *Examples of the Principle*

To return to an earlier example, according to the implicit encoding principle, the reason mental imagery is useful in determining whether or not Thomas Jefferson had a beard is that most people have not previously learned this as an explicit fact about Thomas Jefferson. Similarly, the reason mental images are useful in comparing objects from memory, as suggested by the symbolic distance effect, is that many of those comparisons have not been explicitly made in the past. Imagery seems to be helpful, for example, in determining whether a pineapple is larger than a coconut because few people have previously made this particular comparison. Once the relationship between the two objects is made explicit, as when verbal labels or descriptions are applied, imagery becomes less useful.

Likewise, the reason imagery is used to perform the letter judgment task devised by Brooks is that most people have not explicitly learned where the successive corners are on block letters. The implicit encoding principle states that in such cases, one would need to use imagery to retrieve the information correctly; hence, any task that interferes with imagery would disrupt the retrieval process.

Roger Shepard (1966) has reported a particularly striking example of the implicit encoding principle. Consider the following question: How many windows are there in your house? This is something very few people have ever explicitly learned. Unless you happen to live in a very small house, or one with few windows, you will probably have to imagine looking at each room while counting up the total number of windows, in order to retrieve this information from memory.

1.4.2 *The Dual Coding Hypothesis*

One might wonder why a person would ever really need to use imagery to retrieve information about how an object looks or how a room appears. Surely the essential information must already exist somewhere in memory, in order for one to generate a correct image in the first place. However, the information may never have been "put together" in the right way, which might be accomplished for the first time when one forms an image. Also, there is an important difference between having information stored in memory and having it readily available for retrieval. Unless the information has been explicitly encoded, it may not be accessible as a "known fact," in which case generating an image may be essential to the retrieval process.

There is another reason why mental imagery is particularly useful in retrieving information that was not explicitly encoded. As suggested by the extensive investigations of Allan Paivio (1969, 1979), people may actually use two distinct "codes"—an *imagery* code and a *verbal* code—both to store and to retrieve information. Paivio's experiments showed that these two codes could be used independently to memorize the names of different kinds of words. For example, people tend to use imagery to memorize the names of concrete objects such as "table" or "horse," but not abstract concepts such as "truth" or "beauty." Having a separate imagery code would therefore make it possible to recall information about physical objects that was never encoded using explicit, verbal memorization.

Paivio's dual coding hypothesis also helps to explain why pictures, as a rule, are much easier to remember than words (Shepard 1967; Standing 1973). In recalling pictures, one can use both imagery and verbal codes (Paivio and Csapo 1973). There are, in addition, a number of studies showing that pictures are often *better* recalled over time, an effect known as "hypermnesia," whereas words tend to be forgotten (Erdelyi and Becker 1974; Payne 1986). This would make sense if imagery could be employed, over time, to progressively recover the implicitly encoded visual details in pictures.

1.4.3 Incidental Learning

Perhaps the most direct evidence in support of the implicit encoding principle comes from studies on *incidental learning*. In these types of studies, a person's memory for something is tested unexpectedly. This is in contrast to *intentional learning*, where a person is explicitly told, in advance, that his or her memory will be tested for the presented material. According to the implicit encoding principle, imagery will often be used to retrieve information that was incidentally learned, especially when the information pertains to physical objects or their relationships.

For example, in a study by Peter Sheehan (1971), subjects were presented with a list of nouns referring to either concrete objects or abstract concepts and were told to rate the familiarity of each. From Paivio's work, Sheehan knew that the concrete nouns would elicit more imagery than the abstract nouns and would thus be easier to remember under incidental learning conditions. In support of this prediction, he found that more concrete nouns than abstract nouns were later recognized. This difference was much greater than in an intentional learning task, in which the subjects had been instructed to try to remember the nouns before they were presented. In a related study, Sheehan and Neisser (1969) found that the accuracy of recalling items that were learned incidentally depended on how vividly the subjects imagined the items when trying to recall them. These studies further reveal the importance of using imagery to retrieve information that was not deliberately committed to memory.

1.4.4 Imagery Mnemonics

The role that mental imagery plays in incidental learning is even more apparent when people are instructed to imagine interactions among objects. Gordon Bower (1970) has explored the extent to which imagery facilitates the learning of "paired associates," where one is presented with pairs of unrelated words, is later given the first word in each pair, and is then asked to recall the word that was associated with it. For instance, a person given the word pair "cow-tree" would later be given the word "cow" as a cue and would try to recall the word "tree." Bower found that recall of paired associates was much better when subjects were told to imagine the two objects interacting, than when they were told to form separate images of the objects or simply to memorize their associations. For example, imagining "a cow sitting in a tree" would lead to better recall of the word "tree" when the word "cow" was presented than imagining a cow and a tree separately, or just repeating the words "cow" and "tree" together. What was particularly striking about this technique was that it was equally effective whether or not the subjects *knew* that their memory for the associations would be tested. Imagining that objects are interacting yields recall of the objects that is just as good whether the associations are learned intentionally or incidentally.

An extension of this technique provides an excellent mnemonic device for remembering an entire *list* of items. The method depends on knowing a familiar route with distinctive landmarks along the way. What you do is to take the list of items you want to remember, and imagine a meaningful interaction between the items and each successive landmark along the route. When you wish to recall the items, simply imagine walking along the route and looking at each of the landmarks to mentally "see" the item that was associated with it.

Suppose, for instance, that you wanted to remember a list of food items to pick up at the supermarket. Knowing the major landmarks along the way, you could use imagery to retrieve the list reliably. If the first item was a loaf of bread and the first landmark was a mailbox, you might imagine a loaf of bread in the mailbox with a stamp on it. If the second item was a carton of milk and the second landmark a fire hydrant, you could imagine that the fire hydrant had a stream of milk gushing out of it, and so on. Then, to retrieve the items from memory, you would imagine walking along the route and looking at each of the landmarks. This procedure, called the "method of loci," was invented by the ancient Greeks (see Yates 1966). It, too, is effective whether or not the associations are imagined with the explicit intention of recalling them (Bower 1970).

One explanation for why imagined interactions facilitate the retrieval of objects has to do with something called "encoding specificity" (Tulving and Thomson 1973). Encoding specificity means that physical cues in the learning context are automatically stored along with the items to be remembered, in effect tying memories for those items to the cues. Restoring the learning context, either by observing it directly or recreating it in imagination, thereby facilitates retrieval of the items. In the method of loci, the learning context is the route and its familiar landmarks, and because these landmarks can be easily recalled, the associated items are readily recovered.

There is a common experience that illustrates the use of imagery to retrieve a visual context for the purpose of recalling an incidental event. Have you ever misplaced a pair of glasses or your car keys and found yourself trying to visualize the places where you had recently been? This technique, like the method of loci, is effective because visualizing the appropriate context makes it easier to retrieve associations between the desired items and their physical locations.

Another explanation for the mnemonic effectiveness of forming imagined associations is based on the concept of "depth of processing" (Craik and Lockhart 1972). The "depth" to which something is processed refers to the extent to which one can come up with meaningful associations to an item. This increases the probability of recalling the item, apart from one's intention to remember it (Craik and Tulving 1975). By imagining that objects are interacting in meaningful ways, one would increase the likelihood that the objects could be recalled, even though the interactions may not have been explicitly encoded.

Some researchers, as well as professional mnemonists, have claimed that making the imagined interactions more *bizarre* increases their effectiveness in retrieving memories (O'Brien and Wolford 1982; Lorayne and Lucas 1974). For example, to remember an association between a "dog" and a "bicycle," you might imagine a dog riding a bicycle down the road, instead of imagining a cyclist being chased by a dog. However, a number of studies have failed to find any particular advantage to having imagined bizarre rather than normal interactions (Kroll, Schepeler, and Angin 1986; Nappe and Wollen 1973; Wollen, Weber, and Lowry 1972). Perhaps bizarreness helps indirectly, by making the remembered items more distinctive in memory (McDaniel and Einstein 1986). In any event, the precise role that bizarreness might play in imagery mnemonics remains unclear.

1.4.5 Distinguishing Memories for Real and Imagined Events

A recent experiment from my own laboratory has explored some of the implications of the implicit encoding principle for what has been termed "reality monitoring." This refers to the procedures people use to distinguish memories of events that actually happened from memories of events that were merely imagined (Anderson 1984; Johnson, Raye, Wang, and Taylor 1979). Marcia Johnson and Carol Raye have proposed a theory of reality monitoring that takes into account a wide range of factors that determine how successfully real and imagined events can be distinguished (Johnson and Raye 1981). One prediction that follows from their theory is that memories for real and imagined events should be easier to distinguish whenever the images are difficult to form. The reason is that one can remember more about how an image was generated when it was particularly hard to do so. In contrast, if an image was very easy to form, or was elicited spontaneously, it would be harder to tell whether the event was imagined or actually perceived. Mental images formed under incidental learning conditions should therefore be more confusable with memories of actual experiences, whenever the images require less effort to construct.

Johnson, Gary Shyi, and I tested this prediction using partially drawn geometric patterns that could be "completed" in imagination to make bilaterally asymmetrical forms (Finke, Johnson, and Shyi 1988). These patterns were designed to be visually distinct but difficult to describe. As shown by the examples in figure 1.4, the patterns were presented to the subjects either as whole, completed forms, or as half forms that were divided along the axis of symmetry. Whenever a half form was shown, it was to be imagined as a completed form. The subjects' initial task was to rate the complexity of each of the completed forms, regardless of whether the forms were imagined or presented as complete. This served as a "cover" task for the subsequent memory test. We knew from previous experiments that forms divided along the horizontal axis were much easier to imagine as complete than those divided along the vertical axis. We therefore predicted that there would be more errors in deciding whether the completed form had been seen or imagined as complete when it was vertically symmetrical than when it was horizontally symmetrical.

An unexpected recognition test in the second part of the experiment confirmed this prediction: As shown in figure 1.5, subjects made more errors confusing the presented and imagined forms when

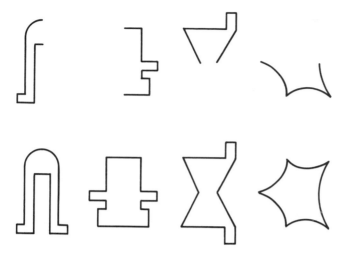

Figure 1.4
Examples of stimuli used in experiments on confusing memories for real and imagined patterns. When the half forms were shown, the subjects were instructed to imagine them as symmetrical, whole forms, or were given no imagery instructions. They were then shown the whole forms and had to recall whether the forms had actually been seen or had merely been imagined as complete. (from Finke, Johnson, and Shyi 1988)

the forms were vertically symmetrical. This effect was not obtained, however, in a control experiment in which the subjects were never given imagery instructions but were simply told to rate the complexity of the forms. These findings suggest that although completing something in imagination might make it easier to remember the item (Kunen, Green, and Waterman 1979), it might also make it harder to determine whether the item had been imagined or perceived. This should be especially true if the images were easy to form, and if one did not explicitly encode the source of the memory.

1.5 Criticisms of Experiments on Image Retrieval

To many readers, these findings might not seem very surprising. After all, almost everyone can recall times when they used imagery to retrieve information about how something looked, or were confused about whether they had actually done something or had imagined doing it. So why bother conducting experiments to validate these experiences? As I mentioned previously, one cannot base a science on mere introspection; it is not a reliable method. In the late nineteenth century, people were trained to introspect in careful and

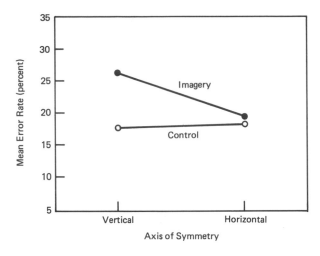

Figure 1.5
Mean error rate for discriminating previously seen whole forms from completed versions of half forms, depending on the axis of symmetry of the forms and on whether or not the subjects were explicitly told to imagine completing the half forms. There were a greater number of memory confusions for imagined completions of the vertically symmetrical forms, which had been judged as easier to imagine. This suggests that memories for imagined and perceived patterns become less distinct as the images become easier to form. (from Finke, Johnson, and Shyi 1988)

systematic ways, but the failure of this method eventually led to the rejection of imagery as a serious research topic (Boring 1950). This might not have happened had these early researchers developed objective methods for verifying the subjectively "obvious" properties of images.

One of the themes of this book is that it is important to rule out alternative explanations for the findings of imagery experiments, even when they do seem intuitively obvious. Moreover, certain issues concerning the nature of imagery may be so subtle that they could never be resolved by introspection alone. These points are illustrated by the following criticisms of the previous experiments.

1.5.1 Critique of the Picture Metaphor
The findings cited in support of the implicit encoding principle show that mental images are distinct from verbal descriptions. They also suggest that images can depict the appearances of physical objects and relationships among them. This might imply that mental images are truly like "pictures" in the mind, but there are serious problems with a literal interpretation of this "picture" metaphor.

Zenon Pylyshyn, a critic of imagery research, has pointed out that mental images differ from pictures in several important respects (Pylyshyn 1973). For one thing, pictures, unlike images, have to be inspected before they can be interpreted. A mental image, in contrast, is always formed according to an intended meaning or interpretation. For example, if you imagine that you are looking at your best friend, you don't have to inspect your image to know that it represents your best friend. The image is already interpreted (see also Chambers and Reisberg 1985; Fodor 1975).

Another problem with the picture metaphor is that images tend to be meaningful and well organized, whereas pictures can be fragmented and meaningless. To use one of Pylyshyn's examples, a mental image would never have an arbitrary piece missing, like a corner torn off a photograph. Rather, images are put together in meaningful, organized ways, and they fade in meaningful, organized ways.

It follows that although images may depict how physical objects look, there is more to an image than just its "pictorial" characteristics. Indeed, if images are formed according to one's interpretations of things, the exact form an image takes can be altered if these interpretations change. Images of your friends can change if, one day, you happen to feel differently about them. Images, unlike photographs, undergo constant change.

In fact, there is a general tendency for *all* memories to change over time (Bartlett 1932). This has been revealed particularly by studies on the formation of "prototypes" in memory, where what tends to be remembered is a kind of "average" appearance for a whole class of items (Franks and Bransford 1971; Posner and Keele 1968, 1970). For example, in recalling what a specific German shepherd looks like, people tend to visualize a typical, average German shepherd. This can lead to a variety of memory distortions, in which natural but missing details are included and atypical but actual details are forgotten.

1.5.2 Evaluating Reports of "Photographic" Memories

These criticisms of the picture metaphor are in sharp contrast to occasional reports in the news media about people who supposedly retrieved the exact details of an event they witnessed while vividly reconstructing the event under hypnosis. Doesn't this imply that some memories are indeed "photographic"? Not necessarily. Many of the details reported under hypnotic regression are, in fact, fabrications or distortions of what actually occurred (Loftus and Loftus

1980). Using hypnosis can facilitate recall insofar as it helps to rein-
state the context in which an event occurred, making the event more
easily retrieved, but it cannot elicit memories that were never fully
established in the first place, or that have already been distorted (see
Sheehan and Tilden 1983).

Another popular misconception is that chess masters have photographic memories, because they can remember complex chess positions accurately and can anticipate the far-reaching consequences of
making a particular sequence of moves. Investigations by Chase and
Simon (1973), however, have shown that chess masters and novices
alike are both very poor at recalling randomly constructed chess
positions. The superior memory of a chess master is restricted to
chess positions that are taken from actual game situations. Evidently,
what is important in becoming a chess master is the ability to visualize meaningful relationships among the pieces, not merely their
physical locations.

A good reason why visual memories are unlikely ever to be truly
"photographic" is that they can be distorted by simply implying to
someone that the event happened in some other way. This has been
shown in a series of studies by Elizabeth Loftus and her colleagues
(see Loftus 1979). In one study, subjects observed a sequence of slides
depicting a traffic accident involving a Datsun and a pedestrian (Loftus, Miller, and Burns 1978). One of the slides showed the Datsun
at either a stop sign or a yield sign. After all the slides were presented, the subjects were asked whether another car had passed the
Datsun at the intersection. For half the subjects, this question referred
to the correct traffic sign, mentioning the "yield" sign or the "stop"
sign, whichever had actually been shown. For the other half, it
mentioned a "yield" sign when there had actually been a stop sign,
and vice versa. Later, the subjects were asked whether they had seen
a stop sign or a yield sign. Twice as many errors were made when
the experimenter had referred to the wrong sign, implying that the
subjects' visual memories had been altered by the misleading verbal
information. (There is, however, some recent evidence that memories
may not always be impaired by these procedures; see McCloskey
and Zaragoza 1985.)

There are, therefore, some limits on the extent to which imagery
can be used to retrieve information about the incidental details of an
event. Although one can employ various mnemonic techniques, such
as those discussed in section 1.4.4, to make it less likely that these
distortions will happen, there is no way to ensure that a visual
memory will be completely accurate or remain unchanged.

1.5.3 *Examples of How Initial Interpretations Distort Visual Memories*

Carmichael, Hogan, and Walter (1932) demonstrated many years ago that the way in which an object is interpreted when it is first presented can influence one's memory for the exact form of the object later on. They showed subjects a set of ambiguous patterns, such as those in figure 1.6, that were labeled according to one of two interpretations. For example, for one group of subjects, the first pattern was labeled as a "crescent moon," and for another group of subjects, as a "letter C." The subjects were later asked to reproduce the patterns from memory. As shown by examples of their drawings in figure 1.7, the subjects' reproductions were strongly influenced by their initial interpretations. If images were really like mental photographs, the exact shapes of the patterns would have been retained, regardless of how they were interpreted.

The distorting effects on visual memory are also seen with highly familiar objects, such as coins. For instance, try drawing a penny without looking at one. Nickerson and Adams (1979) had subjects do this and found that they almost always made significant errors, such as putting the date in the wrong place, including the wrong motto, or having Lincoln's face turned the wrong way. Most of these

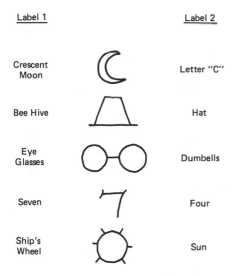

Label 1		Label 2
Crescent Moon		Letter "C"
Bee Hive		Hat
Eye Glasses		Dumbells
Seven		Four
Ship's Wheel		Sun

Figure 1.6
Examples of ambiguous patterns that were presented to subjects and were labeled according to one of two equally plausible interpretations. The subjects were later asked to reconstruct the exact form of the patterns from memory. (from Carmichael, Hogan, and Walter 1932)

Label 1   Label 2

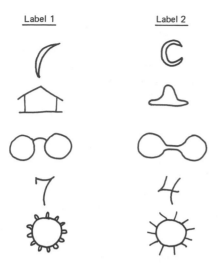

Figure 1.7
Examples of subjects' reconstructions of the patterns shown in figure 1.6, according to how the patterns were initially labeled. The distortions in these reproductions reveal the effects of initial interpretations on visual memories. (from Carmichael, Hogan, and Walter 1932)

errors could be accounted for in terms of erroneous beliefs that the subjects had about the appearance of a penny.

Most people doing imagery research today acknowledge that the picture metaphor should not be taken too literally. The question of current interest is not whether images function in exactly the same way as pictures, but whether images share *any* properties in common with pictures. For example, an image might be generated according to an interpretation of how something is supposed to look, but once generated it could still exhibit visual characteristics, and those characteristics could then be useful in retrieving information about the visual appearances of objects. The implicit encoding principle does not require that an image be an exact reproduction of something in order to serve a useful function in retrieving information. In chapter 5, I will consider at length the extent to which the visual properties of images are functionally distinct from interpretations that are initially given to them.

1.5.4 Spatial vs. Visual Properties of Images
Another criticism that has been leveled at imagery research is that the experiments often fail to distinguish between the *visual* characteristics of an image and its *spatial* characteristics. For instance, people

can close their eyes and have a spatial "awareness" of where things are in a room, without necessarily visualizing how the objects look. Many of the apparent benefits of visual imagery in information retrieval could therefore be due to the spatial properties of images, and not necessarily to their visual properties.

This certainly seems to be true at least for the Brooks study on interference with visualization that was described in section 1.3.2. Recall that Brooks had found that judging the corners of an imagined block letter was more difficult when the responses were given by pointing to visual symbols than when given verbally, whereas the opposite was true when the task involved judging words in sentences. This had suggested that mental images of letters are more like pictures than verbal descriptions.

In the same study, however, Brooks also found interference on the block letter task when the responses were given by *tactually* guided rather than visually guided movements. The subjects were given a cardboard sheet containing a column of holes; they were instructed to close their eyes and to respond "yes" or "no" by marking each of the holes. Giving responses in this manner required that the subjects monitor the spatial locations of the holes, but not their visual appearances. Nevertheless, there was just as much interference in performing the imagery task as when the responses were visually guided.

The Brooks interference effects are therefore more likely due to the common spatial characteristics of imagery and perception than to their common visual characteristics. This was further shown in a recent study by Kerr, Condon, and McDonald (1985), in which subjects performed the imagery tasks devised by Brooks while either sitting down or standing in an unsteady position with their eyes closed. There was more interference when they performed the tasks while standing, which again suggests that the interference is spatial and not visual in nature.

A similar objection can be raised with regard to the symbolic distance effect, discussed in section 1.3.3. Recall that these experiments showed that when people are asked to compare the sizes of two objects from memory, such as a pair of animals, the time it takes them to do so increases as the objects become more similar in size. This implied that the comparisons were being made by visualizing the objects at their appropriate relative sizes.

The difficulty with this conclusion is that the symbolic distance effect has also been obtained when people are asked to compare things from memory that differ along abstract dimensions, where visualization per se would be much less relevant. For example, comparisons of the intelligence and pleasantness of animals also yield the symbolic distance effect (Kerst and Howard 1977; Paivio 1978; Paivio and Marschark 1980), as do comparisons of the relative "goodness" of words denoting abstract concepts (such as "hate" vs. "joy"; see Friedman 1978). These findings show that the symbolic distance effect is not necessarily due to visual comparisons in the mind's eye, but may instead reflect the spatial ordering of information in memory. Specifically, whenever an attribute of something can vary along a continuum, it may be stored along a continuous mental "scale," such that items that are close together on the scale take longer to distinguish during the retrieval process. This would be true whether the attributes are physical characteristics, such as size, or evaluative characteristics, such as "goodness." Thus, whereas the symbolic distance effect does not seem to be explainable in terms of verbal labels or descriptions, it likewise does not seem to be explainable in terms of imagery that is exclusively visual.

What about the mnemonic techniques described previously? Does their effectiveness depend on the visual characteristics of images? An experiment by Ulric Neisser and Nancy Kerr suggests otherwise. They asked subjects to form images of descriptive sentences and to rate the vividness of their imagery, as a cover task for a subsequent test of incidental learning (Neisser and Kerr 1973). In one type of sentence, a pair of objects were related by a pictorial interaction that could be explicitly visualized ("A harp is sitting on top of the torch held up by the Statue of Liberty"). In another type of sentence, the objects were related by a concealed interaction; that is, an interaction that could not be explicitly visualized, but which expressed a spatial connection between the objects ("A harp is hidden inside the torch held up by the Statue of Liberty"). In a third type of sentence, the objects were spatially separated ("Looking from one window, you see the Statue of Liberty; from a window in another wall, you see a harp"). The subjects were then given one of the objects in the sentence (the "Statue of Liberty"), and were asked to recall the other object (the "harp"). The pictorial and concealed interaction images were equally superior to the separate images in recalling the cued items. Neisser and Kerr concluded, therefore, that the effectiveness of images in mnemonic applications stems from their spatial and not their visual characteristics.

The Neisser and Kerr study has been criticized because their instructions to imagine a concealed interaction may not have been effective. For example, subjects may have imagined seeing the harp inside of the torch of the Statue of Liberty, even though it was supposed to have been concealed. In an attempted replication by

Keenan and Moore (1979), when subjects were given instructions that emphasized concealing the objects, pictorial interactions led to better incidental learning than concealed interactions. Kerr and Neisser (1983), in turn, have challenged the Keenan and Moore findings. The issue of whether or not visual imagery is superior to spatial imagery in recalling incidentally learned information is still being debated (Keenan 1983).

It does appear, however, that spatial imagery alone can be sufficient, as shown by studies using congenitally blind subjects. Presumably, these subjects would have little or no visual imagery, but would have normal or superior spatial imagery. Kerr (1983) found that blind and sighted subjects performed equally well on incidental learning tasks similar to the one used by Neisser and Kerr. Other studies have demonstrated that giving imagery instructions to blind subjects can improve their performance in a variety of memory tasks (Jonides, Kahn, and Rozin 1975; Zimler and Keenan 1983). Evidently, spatial images can function adequately in most of these mnemonic techniques.

The validity of the implicit encoding principle really doesn't depend on whether the visual or spatial properties of mental images are being used in retrieving information from memory. The principle applies equally well in either case. Experiments that are better suited for distinguishing the visual and spatial properties of images will be considered in the next chapter. In chapter 3, the spatial characteristics of images will be considered at length.

1.5.5 Propositional Theories
A more serious objection to the implicit encoding principle comes from proponents of propositional theories. These theories are based on the idea that there is a single, abstract "propositional" code underlying all types of memory (Anderson and Bower 1973). Propositions are neither visual nor verbal; instead, they specify formal relationships among concepts and their associated properties. For example, the sentence "An apple is red" would be stored as an abstract proposition that links together the concept "apple" with the property "red." Similarly, memories for how a person looks would be stored as a set of abstract propositions specifying all of the features of the person.

One argument for the necessity of an abstract propositional code in memory is that verbal and visual information has to be connected in some way. It would be very inefficient to store information permanently in two separate codes, as in Paivio's dual-coding theory (see section 1.4.2), with one code always having to be translated into the other. Rather, it makes more sense to have a single underlying memory code, from which information can be translated into an image or a sentence when needed, and vice versa. For example, experiments by Potter and Falconer (1975) have shown that it takes the same amount of time to understand words and pictures of objects, even though words can be named more rapidly than pictures. Such findings suggest that a single memory code is used to interpret an object's meaning, regardless of the way the object is initially represented.

In criticizing the picture metaphor, Pylyshyn (1973) advocated a propositional theory to explain the findings of imagery experiments. He argued that these findings are better accounted for in terms of the propositions that must have been used in constructing the images than in terms of the pictorial properties of the images. Note that this is separate from the issue of whether mental images can be distinguished from verbal descriptions. Propositions are not made up simply of words or sentences. If they were, it would be hard to explain why people can often form images of things that are difficult to describe.

If propositional theories are correct, forming an image would be useful in retrieving information from memory only insofar as it makes the relevant propositions more accessible to the retrieval process, and not because people actually depend on the visual or spatial properties of images. In other words, there would be nothing in the structure of the image itself that is crucial for retrieving the desired information. For example, imagining that two objects are interacting may be helpful because it establishes a greater number of propositions relating the two objects, and not because the visual or spatial properties of the image contribute directly to the retrieval process. The implicit encoding principle may simply describe the conditions under which it is easier to make contact with these underlying propositions.

1.6 Distinguishing Images and Propositions

What kinds of experiments would distinguish between whether mental images or propositions were being used to retrieve information about an object and its features? Some exceedingly clever methods for doing so were developed by Stephen Kosslyn. He began by considering the different types of predictions that a propositional theory would make and a theory that assumed that the pictorial properties of images were actually being used in the retrieval process. Kosslyn reasoned that the particular *size* at which an image is formed ought to matter if the information were retrieved by "inspecting" the properties of an image, but not if all one did was make contact with the relevant underlying propositions.

1.6.1 The Effects of Image Size in Information Retrieval

To test this idea, Kosslyn (1975) instructed subjects to imagine looking at an animal, such as a rabbit, next to either an elephant or a fly (see figure 1.8). The subjects were then given the names of animal parts (such as eyes, nose, ears, etc.), and they were to respond "yes" or "no" to indicate whether the named part could be found on their image of the animal. Kosslyn's intuition was that the parts would be found more quickly when the animal was imagined next to a fly, because the animal could then be imagined at a subjectively larger size. If you try to imagine a rabbit next to an elephant, for example, the rabbit "appears" small and its features are hard to resolve. When a rabbit is imagined next to a fly, however, its features seem larger and are easier to detect.

A potential problem with this kind of procedure is that a person might still be drawing on propositional knowledge about the actual relative sizes of the animals, instead of relying on his or her images. To meet this objection, Kosslyn included an important control in his experiment. In one condition, the subjects were told to imagine the animal next to an elephant or a fly at their true relative sizes. In another condition, they were told to imagine the animal next to an elephant that was the size of a fly, or next to a fly that was the size

Figure 1.8
An imagery task designed to measure the effects of varying the subjective size of an image on the time it takes to retrieve information from the image. Subjects were instructed to imagine an animal, such as a rabbit, next to either an elephant or a fly and then to try to "find" parts of the animal using their image. In a control condition, they were instructed to imagine the animal next to a fly that was the size of an elephant or next to an elephant that was the size of a fly. (from Kosslyn 1983)

of an elephant. If what matters is the size at which an image of an animal is actually formed, and not the true size of the animal, response times for detecting parts of the imagined animal should be shorter when the animal is imagined next to the fly in the first condition, but next to the elephant in the second condition.

This is just what Kosslyn found. As shown in figure 1.9, reaction time for verifying the presence of a named part in the imagined animal was faster when the context animal was imagined next to it at a small subjective size. In other words, the time it takes to retrieve information from an image decreases as the image is formed at a subjectively larger size, apart from the true size of the object being imagined. The "pictorial" properties of images can thus be used in the retrieval process, and can be distinguished from abstract, propositional forms of knowledge about an object's actual size. (See also the related findings by Kosslyn and Alper 1977, and Ritchey and Beal 1980.)

1.6.2 Contrasting Size and Association Strength
Propositional theories are, however, sufficiently flexible that some versions of them could still account for these findings. As John

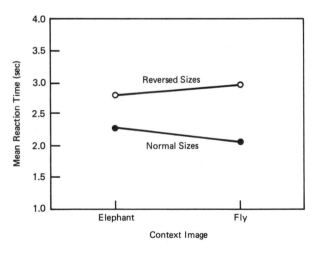

Figure 1.9
Mean reaction time to verify that an imagined animal contained parts that were named, depending on which context animal was imagined next to it and on whether the context animals were to be imagined at their normal or reversed sizes. The differences in response times indicate that it takes less time to find parts on an image that can be formed at a subjectively larger size. (from Kosslyn 1975)

Anderson (1978) has argued, all one has to do is to make certain assumptions about how propositional knowledge is retrieved in order to make it look like information is being read off a mental image. As an analogy, one could pretend to be looking at a map when actually reading descriptions of how the map looks, simply by adjusting one's response times to simulate a visual search.

A more convincing demonstration would be to show that an imagery theory can sometimes make predictions that are directly *opposite* those that any reasonable propositional theory would make. Following up on his previous work, Kosslyn (1976) compared the effect of varying the size of the parts of imagined animals with the effect of varying the association strength between the animals and their parts. Association strength refers to how strongly two things are related in memory; it can be thought of as reflecting the extent to which propositions relating the two items have been established. Virtually all propositional models would predict that the greater the association strength, the less time it would take to retrieve one of the items given the other. For example, given the word "cat," the word "mouse" would be more readily retrieved from memory than the word "house," because there are more propositions linking the concepts "cat" and "mouse."

In his follow-up experiments, Kosslyn asked subjects to verify from memory parts of animals that were either strongly associated with the animal but relatively small in size (for instance, the "claws" of a cat), or were weakly associated with the animal but relatively large in size (the "head" of a cat). In other words, he pitted association strength directly against size in the retrieval process. As shown in figure 1.10, when the subjects reported not having used imagery to perform the task, their verification times were shorter for the small, high-association parts, consistent with the predictions of a propositional model. However, when the subjects were instructed to use imagery to find the parts, and reported having done so, their verification times were shorter for the large, low-association parts. This is consistent with the predictions of a model that assumes that the pictorial properties of an image can also be used to retrieve information.

As you can see, trying to distinguish images from propositions is a complex issue, one that could hardly be resolved using introspection alone. On the contrary, carefully controlled experiments are needed to rule out alternative explanations for most imagery findings. This is what makes the scientific study of imagery so exciting.

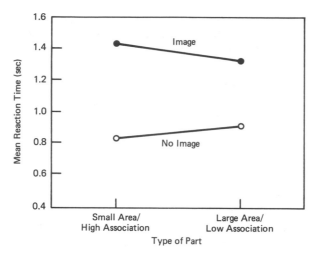

Figure 1.10
Mean reaction time to verify, from memory, that an animal had a designated part, depending on whether the part was small but highly associated with the name of the animal or large but weakly associated with the name of the animal, and depending on whether subjects reported using imagery when responding. The difference in these functions suggests that the size of a part is what matters when imagery is used to retrieve information from memory, whereas association strength is what matters when imagery is not used. (from Kosslyn 1976)

1.7 Summary and Conclusions

The experiments discussed in this chapter have shown that mental images can be distinguished from verbal descriptions and, to some extent, from propositions that might underlie the formation of an image. Most of these findings can be accounted for by the implicit encoding principle, which states that imagery would be particularly useful in recalling information about objects and their relationships whenever the information has not been explicitly encoded. This principle is supported particularly by studies that have explored the role that imagery plays in incidental learning. Experiments on memory distortions, however, suggest that the principle may be limited if an image changes considerably over time.

1.8 Further Explorations

1.8.1 Recommendations for Further Reading
The classic reference for the role that imagery plays in memory is Paivio's *Imagery and Verbal Processes* (1979). A more recent book by

Richardson (1980) also provides a good summary of research on imagery and memory. An article by Bugelski (1970) reviews historical reasons why the study of imagery was long ignored in American psychology.

A good introduction to the "imagery–propositional" debate can be found in articles by Hayes-Roth (1979), Kolers and Smythe (1979), Kosslyn and Pomerantz (1977), Paivio (1977), and Pylyshyn (1981). This debate has lost some of its appeal over the years, and criticisms of imagery research have begun to take other forms.

1.8.2 Individual Differences
One of the first things that one discovers in doing imagery research is that people differ in their imagery skills. Some claim to be able to form clear and vivid images at will; others claim to have little if any imagery ability. Although I will not consider individual differences to any great extent in this book, some discussion of this topic is in order.

A number of scales have been developed to measure individual differences in the vividness of imagery, the most popular being the self-report scales of Betts (1909) and Marks (1973). Self-report scales have also been developed to assess one's ability to control images, as distinct from the ability to form vivid images (Gordon 1949). Although these and other self-report measures have been firmly established in imagery research (see reviews by Marks 1983; White, Sheehan, and Ashton 1977), they are not always reliable and can be influenced by other factors, such as social desirability (see Di Vesta, Ingersoll, and Sunshine 1971).

Perhaps the most successful self-report scale is Marks's (1973) Vividness of Visual Imagery Questionnaire (VVIQ). This consists of descriptions of visual scenes that subjects try to imagine (e.g., "The sun is rising above the horizon into a hazy sky"); they then rate the vividness of their imagery on a 5-point scale. The ratings can range from "Perfectly clear and as vivid as normal vision" to "No image at all, you just 'know' that you are thinking of the object." The VVIQ has been useful in predicting individual differences in recognizing and recalling pictures (Gur and Hilgard 1975; Marks 1973), as well as performance on a variety of other imagery tasks (reviewed in Marks 1983). Unless stated otherwise, all references to individual differences in imagery vividness in this book will refer to the VVIQ.

1.8.3 Eidetic Imagery
An exception to my arguments against images being "photographic" comes from studies on *eidetic* imagery. It is often claimed that certain

people (usually children) have the ability to retain extremely clear and detailed images of recently viewed pictures and scenes. Haber (1979), in particular, has conducted many investigations of eidetic imagery, and believes that it is qualitatively different from ordinary forms of imagery, although extremely rare. Other researchers have been critical of these claims, and have concluded that eidetic imagery is not really a distinct form of imagery (Gray and Gummerman 1975). At present, imagery researchers seem divided on this issue.

1.8.4 Visual Rehearsal

People typically use a verbal or "acoustic" code to rehearse information in short-term memory (e.g., Conrad 1964), as when trying to remember a telephone number long enough to write it down. However, a number of studies have shown that information can also be retained in short-term memory using a "visual" code (Posner et al. 1969; Kroll et al. 1970; Seamon 1976). This "visual" form of rehearsal is clearly distinct from "speech" imagery, where one mentally repeats the sounds of words or letters (Anderson 1982; Weber and Castleman 1970).

Using imagery to visually rehearse information may improve one's memory for that information. Graefe and Watkins (1980), for example, found that pictures could be recalled more accurately when subjects were encouraged to mentally rehearse them during a brief retention period. Imagery may therefore facilitate memory not only by helping to retrieve visual information, as suggested by many of the experiments in this chapter, but also by helping to retain the information temporarily so that it can be more effectively encoded into memory.

Chapter 2
Visual Characteristics of Mental Images

The previous chapter left open the question of how one might distinguish the visual characteristics of images from their spatial characteristics. This will be the topic of the present chapter, which will consider, in particular, the relationship between mental imagery and visual perception.

2.1 The Visual Field in Mental Imagery

One of the important things about visual perception is that the "field" of vision is limited. We can see objects clearly only when they fall within a certain region of space, called the *visual field*, depending on where our eyes are pointed. For example, hold up your index finger directly in front of you at arm's distance. Now, keeping your gaze fixed straight ahead, and your arm extended, slowly move your finger around to the side of your head. There will be a point where you can no longer see your finger; you will simply "know" where it is, without being able to detect it visually. Is there a similar kind of restricted visual field in mental imagery? If so, how would you measure it?

2.1.1 Demonstrating "Overflow" in Visualization

In Kosslyn's (1975) studies on the effects of varying the size of images, which were discussed in section 1.6, he noticed that an image of an animal would begin to "overflow" whenever the animal was imagined too closely or at too large a size. For example, try to imagine that you are looking at an elephant standing far away next to a tree on a distant hill. It should be fairly easy to keep the entire elephant "visible" all at once in your mind's eye. Now imagine zooming in on the elephant, until it seems close enough to touch. Is there a point at which the elephant can no longer be mentally "seen" all at once, where your image begins to "overflow"?

If the visual size at which an image can be formed is limited, this would have two implications. First, it would imply that it is not always easier to retrieve information from a subjectively larger image, as was previously suggested (see section 1.6.1). If one attempts to imagine an object at too close a distance, some of the object's features may fall outside the imagery field. Instead, there ought to be an *optimal* size for forming an image, just below the point of overflow. Second, having a limit on the visual size of an image suggests one way in which visual imagery can be distinguished from spatial imagery.

Imagining the spatial location of an object would not be restricted to any particular region of space relative to the observer; a person can imagine that objects are located behind his or her head, for example (Attneave and Farrar 1977; Attneave and Pierce 1978). In contrast, visualization seems to require that one mentally "look" at or near an object.

2.1.2 Measuring the Imagery Field

Kosslyn (1978) attempted to measure the maximum visual field within which an object can be imagined. He devised several methods for doing so, only one of which will be described here. Subjects were first trained in estimating distances to the end wall in a hallway. They were then given drawings of animals or geometric shapes to study until they could visualize the drawings accurately. Following this, they were asked to imagine the drawings projected onto the wall, to imagine walking towards the drawings until their image overflowed, and to estimate the distance from the wall when this occurred. The term "overflow" was defined as the point where all parts of the image could not be kept in sharp focus at the same time.

Using this technique, Kosslyn found that the visual field in imagery had a diameter of about 20–30 degrees of visual angle. If you hold your hands outstretched in front of you, this would correspond to about 6–8 inches of separation between your hands. These estimates were calculated by plotting the size of the drawing, as measured by the length of its diagonal (or longest axis), against the distance at which the image was judged to overflow. For example, as shown in figure 2.1, when the imagined stimulus was a solid rectangle, the estimated distance at which overflow occurred increased in proportion to the length of the rectangle's diagonal, indicating a visual field of around 20 degrees. In the same study, Kosslyn also measured the approximate shape of the imagery field by having subjects repeat the distance estimation task using a ruler that was imagined vertically, horizontally, or diagonally. The estimated diameter of the imagery

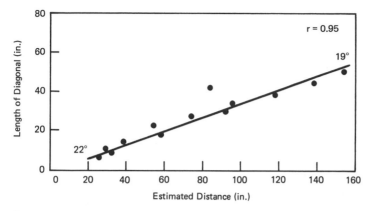

Figure 2.1
Length of diagonal of rectangles that subjects imagined walking toward, and the estimated distance at which their images of the rectangles began to "overflow." The proportional increase in the estimated distance with increasing length of the diagonal suggests that images overflow within a constant visual angle. (from Kosslyn 1978)

field was about 30 degrees in each case, suggesting that the field is circular.

Other methods have been employed to try to measure the size of the imagery field. Weber and Malmstrom (1979) instructed subjects to visualize words on a screen and then to point to the mentally projected locations of the first and last letters in the imagined words. In another condition, they were told simply to move their eyes between the locations of the imagined letters, and changes in their eye positions were recorded. Both of these measures indicated that the words were visualized within visual angles that averaged about 8 degrees across. This is smaller than the estimates for the diameter of the imagery field reported by Kosslyn, perhaps owing to the greater amount of visual detail that would have to be imagined in the Weber and Malmstrom task (see Kosslyn 1980).

These findings provide empirical evidence that something analogous to a visual field does exist in mental imagery. What this means, for example, is that you could not imagine "seeing" an object in front of you and behind you at exactly the same time, just as you could not simultaneously observe the two objects. But these findings are also limited. It is well known, for example, that the visual field in perception is much larger than these estimates for the size of the imagery field, extending to 100 degrees and beyond, and is not circular, but elliptical (Aulhorn and Harms 1972). More recent imagery experiments, however, suggest that the imagery field is actually quite similar to the field of vision in perception, in spite of these discrepancies.

2.2. Visual Resolution for the Features of Images

In perception, how far into the visual periphery the features of an object can be seen depends both on the size of the features and on how closely spaced the features are. As a rule, features that are large or are spaced far apart can be seen farther into the visual periphery. For example, it is easier to see a cat than a spider using peripheral vision, and easier to see a person who is standing alone than one who is in the middle of a crowd. How easily the features of an object can be resolved, termed *visual resolution* or *acuity*, would thus determine the effective size of the visual field.

Visual resolution is typically measured using *psychophysical* techniques, which are designed to establish lawful relations between the physical characteristics of a stimulus and the sensations that those characteristics elicit (Baird 1970; Stevens 1975). In applying these techniques to measure visual resolution, one often varies the distance between simple features (such as dots or bars), and determines how far into the visual periphery the features can be extended before a person can no longer tell them apart. The usual finding is that the field of resolution expands as the spacing between the features increases (Riggs 1965). A similar method makes use of letters or geometric forms and varies the overall size of the patterns, in which case the field of resolution enlarges as the pattern size increases (Johnson, Keltner, and Balestrery 1978).

2.2.1 Measuring Visual Acuity in Imagery

Kosslyn and I created variations of these psychophysical techniques to obtain a better measure of the extent to which imagined features could be visually resolved, and to compare directly the fields of resolution in imagery and perception (Finke and Kosslyn 1980). Our method is illustrated in figure 2.2. In the perception task, the subjects were shown a pair of dots in a square field at the center of a large screen, on which horizontal and vertical axes were drawn. They were to move their eyes along each of the axes to find the place where the two dots could no longer be resolved peripherally. By moving their eyes away from the dot pattern, they effectively moved the pattern farther into the peripheral regions of their visual field; whereas by moving their eyes toward the pattern, they effectively moved it towards the point of fixation. Eye position was controlled using a

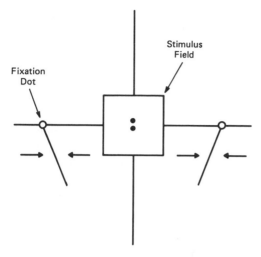

Figure 2.2
Technique used to measure visual resolution in imagery. Subjects imagined a pair of dots at the center of the stimulus field and then used a movable fixation point to shift their gaze along the horizontal and vertical axes of the display, until they could no longer visually distinguish the dots in their images. (from Finke and Kosslyn 1980)

movable pointer that had a small fixation dot attached to it. When the point of limiting resolution was found, the experimenter measured the distance from the fixation point to the center of the pattern. These estimates were then averaged to obtain a measure of the size and general shape of the perceptual fields. By varying the distance between the two dots, Kosslyn and I were able to determine how the fields of resolution varied as the dots became harder or easier to discriminate.

For the imagery task, the subjects made corresponding judgments on mental images of the dot patterns. They first practiced visualizing the patterns by inspecting them, forming an image, and then comparing their image to the actual pattern. When making judgments of resolution in imagery, they were first instructed to visualize the appropriate pattern at the center of a blank stimulus field, where the dot patterns had actually been shown in the perception task. They were then asked to notice changes in the visual "appearance" of their images as they kept their image fixed at the center of the screen, while moving their eyes along the horizontal and vertical axes. In this way, they were to mentally "move" their images into the visual periphery and to find the point where they could no longer visually distinguish the imagined dots. The experimenter emphasized the distinction between the spatial characteristics of an image (imagining where the dots were located), and its explicit visual characteristics (imagining how the dots "looked").

Changes in the estimated dimensions of the fields of resolution, as the distance separating the dots varied, are presented in figure 2.3. The shapes of these functions were statistically equivalent: Although the imagery fields were smaller, on the average, than the perceptual fields, they increased with increasing separation distance in the same way. In addition, the imagery fields were approximately the same shape as the perceptual fields; they were elongated horizontally and were larger below the point of fixation than above. When subjects who were screened for having highly vivid imagery were considered separately, the imagery fields were the same size as the perceptual fields, averaging 90 × 77 degrees.

A control experiment, in which subjects were shown the same stimuli and asked to estimate where the limits of resolution would be in the imagery condition, was performed to assess whether these results could have been easily guessed. The control subjects correctly guessed that the imagery fields should increase as one increases the separation distance, but they did not guess the more subtle findings, such as the precise form of the functions relating field size to sepa-

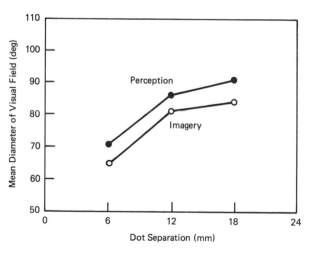

Figure 2.3
Mean diameter of the visual field within which pairs of dots could still be distinguished as the distance separating the dots increased, when the dots were imagined and actually perceived. The correspondence between the two functions suggests that constraints on visual resolution in imagery are similar to those in perception. (from Finke and Kosslyn 1980)

ration distance, or the actual shape of the fields. Thus, only the most obvious characteristics of the imagery fields could be attributed to guessing strategies on the part of the subjects.

Howard Kurtzman and I subsequently found similar results for other kinds of stimulus variations (Finke and Kurtzman 1981a). Using stimuli that consisted of three concentric circles, forming "bull's-eye" targets, we varied both the area and the relative contrast of the patterns. The subjects were now instructed to judge when all three parts of the observed or imagined pattern could no longer be visually resolved. Equivalent functions relating increasing field size to increasing pattern area were obtained in the imagery and perception conditions, and the fields were approximately the same shape, measuring, on the average, 74 × 55 degrees. There was, however, an important difference between these fields: whereas the size of the perceptual fields was markedly influenced when the contrast of the patterns was lowered, this was not true for the imagery fields. Again, control subjects were unable to guess these results.

On the surface, these findings appear to conflict with those of Kosslyn's (1978) study on measuring the size of the imagery field. Recall that Kosslyn had found that the imagery field was circular and was considerably smaller than the fields obtained by either Finke and Kosslyn (1980) or Finke and Kurtzman (1981a). In a further experiment, Kosslyn and I were able to resolve this discrepancy. We found that measures of image overflow reveal not the extent to which visual resolution is possible in imagery, *but the extent to which attention can be distributed across the imagery field* (Finke and Kosslyn 1980). The subjects were first taught to make image resolution judgments with their eyes closed. To do this, they were taught to move the index finger of one hand along the horizontal and vertical axes on the screen, imagining that they were looking at this finger, while keeping the index finger of their other hand at the center of the screen, imagining that the dot pattern remained fixed at that position. The results for this "eyes closed" condition corresponded to those for the condition, described earlier, in which the subjects had kept their eyes opened and had systematically varied their eye fixation. Next, they were told to place both index fingers at the center of the screen, to imagine a dot pattern on *each* finger, and to move their fingers simultaneously away from the center of the screen while keeping their eyes closed and their mental "gaze" straight ahead, until they could no longer imagine "seeing" all of the dots in both of the patterns at the same time. This task required that the subjects distribute their attention *across* the imagery field, as they would have had to do in

Kosslyn's overflow study. The results confirmed this expectation: the imagery fields were now circular and about 30 degrees across, corresponding to the results of the overflow experiments.

2.2.2 Spatial Frequency Resolution in Imagery

Kurtzman and I later refined and extended these methods to develop a general procedure for mapping out the entire visual field in mental imagery (Finke and Kurtzman 1981b). Studies in visual psychophysics frequently use bar gratings as stimuli, and a common finding is that visual resolution for such gratings decreases as their fundamental *spatial frequency* increases (Campbell and Robson 1968). Spatial frequency can be thought of as a measure of the density of bars in the gratings; technically, it is expressed as the number of "cycles" of dark bars alternating with light bars per degree of visual angle. We wanted to see whether changes in the spatial frequency of bar gratings would also affect visual resolution in imagery. Using stimuli that have been employed extensively in perception experiments is a strongly recommended procedure when trying to establish similarities between imagery and perception (Banks 1981).

As shown in figure 2.4, the viewing screen contained eight "spokes" extending radially outward from a centrally positioned, circular stimulus field, denoting the horizontal, vertical, and diagonal axes. The stimulus field was divided in half; the two halves contained a bar grating of identical spatial frequency (1, 3, or 9 cycles/degree), but opposite orientation (horizontal or vertical). The subjects' task was to determine when the two halves of the stimulus field could no longer be distinguished, as they shifted their gaze along each of the axes. This would happen, presumably, when the spatial frequencies in the gratings could no longer be resolved. This procedure has the advantage that the criterion for judging resolution is the same for all kinds of patterns that might be contained in the two halves of the stimulus field. In the perception condition, the bar gratings were present at all times; in the imagery condition, the subjects were instructed to visualize the gratings within a blank stimulus field. Figure 2.5 shows that there was an equivalent drop-off in resolution in the two conditions as the spatial frequency of the gratings increased, and that the imagery fields were the same size as the perceptual fields. As figure 2.6 shows, the fields of resolution in the two conditions were virtually identical in shape as well, exhibiting a similar horizontal elongation and vertical asymmetry. Control subjects were once again unable to predict the form of the acuity functions or the actual shape of the imagery fields.

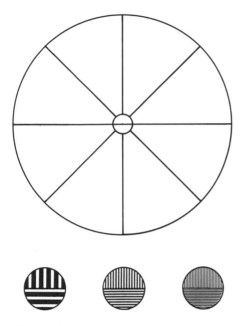

Figure 2.4
Stimuli and display used to measure spatial frequency resolution in imagery. Subjects imagined the two gratings in each stimulus within the blank circular field at the center of the display and then found the point along each radial line where they could no longer tell the gratings apart. These measures defined "fields of resolution" for the imagined gratings. (from Finke and Kurtzman 1981b)

2.2.3 Evidence for an Oblique Effect in Imagery

Pennington and Kosslyn (reported in Kosslyn 1980) have found evidence for an *oblique effect* in mental imagery. The oblique effect refers to the well-documented finding that lines in bar gratings are more difficult to resolve when the gratings are oriented diagonally than when they are oriented horizontally or vertically (Appelle 1972; Campbell, Kulikowski, and Levinson 1966). In the Pennington and Kosslyn study, subjects were first trained to imagine bar gratings that were oriented either vertically or diagonally. They were then instructed to imagine that they were walking away from the gratings and to estimate the distance at which the gratings began to blur. The majority of the subjects reported that the diagonal gratings seemed to blur at a subjectively closer distance than the vertical gratings, suggesting that the diagonal gratings were harder to resolve. Control subjects, merely given a description of the procedures, were not able to guess these results.

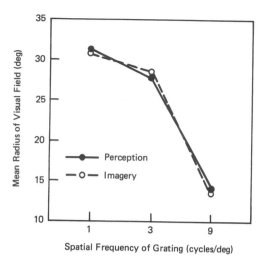

Figure 2.5
Mean radius of fields of resolution as the spatial frequency of the gratings increased, when the gratings were imagined and perceived. The equivalent functions in the two conditions indicate that imagery and perception share similar constraints on spatial frequency resolution. (from Finke and Kurtzman 1981b)

2.2.4 *The Problem of Experimenter Bias*
One criticism that can be made of the foregoing studies is that the experimenters might have given the subjects subtle cues for how to respond during the testing procedures, since they were in continual contact with the subjects. Psychology experiments are frequently susceptible to the effects of experimenter "bias" (e.g., Rosenthal 1976), or to the "demand characteristics" of the experimental procedures (Orne 1962). Their possible effect on image acuity experiments must therefore be considered, especially since the subjects in these experiments may have found the image judgment tasks somewhat puzzling or ambiguous. In contrast, experimenter bias is less of a problem in the information retrieval experiments discussed in the previous chapter, where subjects weren't being asked to judge the quality of their images.

Margaret Intons-Peterson (1983) has reported that the expectations of an experimenter can influence at least some of the results of image acuity experiments. She repeated the Finke and Kurtzman (1981a) study on the effects of varying pattern size and contrast, using experimenters who were led to expect that the imagery fields would either be larger or smaller than the perceptual fields. These expectations were reinforced by training the experimenters with confed-

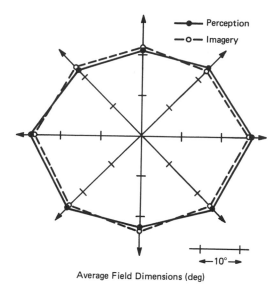

Perception
Imagery

←—10°—→

Average Field Dimensions (deg)

Figure 2.6
Average dimensions of the fields of resolution when the gratings were imagined and perceived. The similar dimensions in the two conditions again suggest that imagery and perception share similar constraints on spatial frequency resolution. (from Finke and Kurtzman 1981b)

erate subjects who simulated these outcomes. When the biased experimenters then conducted the image acuity experiment on naive subjects, the results partially reflected their expectations: the imagery fields were smaller than the perceptual fields when the experimenter expected them to be smaller, but were just as large as the perceptual fields when the experimenter expected them to be larger. Intons-Peterson and White (1981) have also reported that the imagery fields tend to be smaller when the experimenter is naive about the expected outcomes.

Do these results invalidate the findings of the previous image acuity experiments? There are reasons to think that they do not. For instance, it remains to be shown whether experimenter bias can influence the *form* of the function relating image acuity to the size of a pattern. What Intons-Peterson has shown, in effect, is that the "height" or *intercept* of an image acuity function can be influenced by experimenter bias. This could be due to motivational factors alone; subjects may simply form better images when encouraged to do so by the experimenter. The fact that the imagery fields never *exceeded* the perceptual fields, despite the experimenter's expectations, supports this interpretation. In assessing whether imagery acuity is like perceptual acuity, the important thing is the correspondence between the forms of the acuity functions, not the relative height of the functions.

Another argument against attributing the findings of these experiments to experimenter bias is that certain characteristics of the imagery fields were totally *unexpected*. For example, the eccentricity of the imagery fields was slightly but consistently less than that of the perceptual fields, for reasons that have remained unclear (see figure 2.6; see also Finke and Kurtzman 1981c). The finding that changes in pattern contrast have little effect on the imagery fields was also unanticipated. Imagery researchers, in fact, have often pointed to such unexpected results as evidence that the findings of imagery experiments are not simply artifacts of the experimenter's expectations (Kosslyn, Pinker, Smith, and Shwartz 1979).

2.2.5 The Problem of "Tacit" Knowledge

Although the control experiments in these studies rule out simple guessing strategies as an explanation for the findings, they do not rule out the use of propositional knowledge about perceptual acuity (see section 1.5.5). The reason is that propositional knowledge cannot always be retrieved directly from memory. Sometimes, it is only available when a person is performing a specific task; in such cases, it is referred to as "tacit" knowledge (see Polanyi 1962).

Pylyshyn (1981, 1984) has suggested that tacit knowledge about perceptual and physical processes may govern the results of many imagery experiments. This is a difficult criticism to address. In principle, any similarity between imagery and perception *could* be attributed to tacit knowledge. For instance, the precise manner in which visual acuity changes as the size of an object changes, and as the object is moved into the visual periphery, could conceivably be stored as tacit knowledge, given a lifetime of having observed objects in the visual field. This knowledge might then influence how people perform in an image acuity task.

Toward the end of the previous chapter, I discussed Kosslyn's experiments on distinguishing images and propositions in information retrieval, in which image size was contrasted with association strength (section 1.6.2). This strategy won't work here, because the tacit knowledge is allegedly *about* the visual properties of images. There are, however, two other strategies that could conceivably rule out tacit knowledge. One would be to show that the visual characteristics of images are not *always* the same as those of visually perceived objects, in which case one would then have to explain why tacit knowledge exists for some visual characteristics but not others. For example, the subtle, unexpected differences between imagery and perceptual acuity discussed in section 2.2.4, which argued against the possibility of experimenter bias, are also difficult to account for in terms of tacit knowledge. The other strategy is to try to find correspondences between imagery and perception that are so unusual or unnatural that tacit knowledge would never have been acquired. Both of these strategies were employed in the experiments to follow. Before describing these experiments, I shall first discuss our second imagery principle.

2.3 The Principle of Perceptual Equivalence

The second principle addresses visual correspondences between forming mental images and perceiving real objects and events. This principle of *perceptual equivalence* may be expressed as follows:

Imagery is functionally equivalent to perception to the extent that similar mechanisms in the visual system are activated when objects or events are imagined as when the same objects or events are actually perceived.

According to this principle, the origins of which can be traced to the "cell assembly" theory of Donald Hebb (1968), the visual properties of images can be explained in terms of the operating characteristics of neural mechanisms that form the basis for visual perception. I propose that the principle accounts for most of the findings on image acuity. Studies in the neurophysiology of vision have found, for example, that certain cells in the visual cortex are specialized for detecting bar-shaped features of particular width and orientation (Hubel and Wiesel 1977; Schiller, Finlay, and Volman 1976), while others specialize in detecting the spatial frequencies of bar gratings (Maffei and Fiorentini 1977). It is generally believed that these cells impose restrictions on our ability to resolve fine details in the visual field. For instance, neural units that only respond to large, thick features, or to low spatial frequencies, would not allow for the resolution of fine details. These types of cells receive most of the information from the visual periphery, which explains why acuity falls off as objects are observed at increasingly more peripheral regions of the visual field. Similarly, the oblique effect is thought to result from an impoverished population of cortical bar detectors selectively tuned to obliquely oriented stimuli. *If these same neural units were also activated during visualization, they would, accordingly, impose similar restrictions on visual resolution in imagery.*

2.3.1 Detecting Probes on Imagined Features

Podgorny and Shepard (1978) conducted a set of experiments that support the principle of perceptual equivalence, while also addressing the criticisms of experimenter bias and tacit knowledge. The subjects' task was to indicate whether small probes appeared on or off block letters that were formed by darkening in squares on a 5 × 5 grid (see figure 2.7). In the perception condition, the letters were actually presented just before the probes appeared. In the imagery condition, the letters were designated verbally, and the subjects were to visualize the letters in the appropriate cells of an empty 5 × 5 grid. Reaction times for judging the probes in each condition varied in the same way with changes in the size and shape of the letters and the probe locations. As shown in figure 2.8, the reaction times increased at the same rate with increasing number of squares making up the letters. In addition, reaction times in each condition were shorter when the probes fell on the intersection of two bar-shaped segments of the same letter (as, for example, in the upper left-hand corner square of the block letter F) than when they fell only on a single bar-shaped segment. The imagined letters were thus visually equivalent to the perceived letters. Podgorny and Shepard proposed that this equivalence could be explained if similar types of neural units in the visual system, sensitive to bar-shaped features, are activated whenever letters are imagined or observed.

The Podgorny and Shepard experiments are much less susceptible to the possible effects of experimenter bias, as the experimenter was

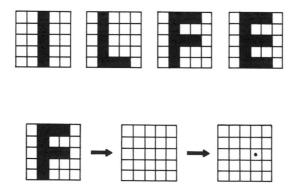

Figure 2.7
Example of square grids and block letters used in experiments on detecting probes on presented and imagined patterns. The subjects had to say whether or not the probes appeared on any square that was a part of the pattern. (from Podgorny and Shepard 1978)

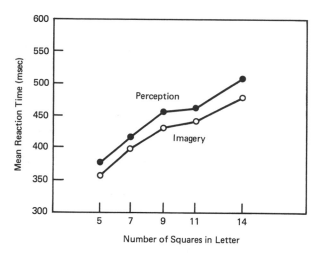

Figure 2.8
Mean reaction time to respond to probes on perceived and imagined letters, as the number of squares making up the letters increased. The similar functions suggest an equivalence between imagined and perceived shapes. (from Podgorny and Shepard 1978)

not in contact with the subjects during the testing procedures. The complex patterns of reaction times to the probes also make it unlikely that tacit knowledge was responsible for these findings. It is highly improbable that the subjects would have learned how reaction times are supposed to vary under these very unnatural visual conditions. More recently, Podgorny and Shepard (1983) have found that the probe detection times in imagery and perception covary with subtle variations in the visual compactness of the forms, and not merely with the number of squares making up the forms—which further argues against a tacit knowledge account, or one based on the intentional adjusting of response latencies.

2.3.2 Levels of Perceptual Equivalence
A fundamental question concerning apparent equivalences between imagery and perception is whether these equivalences would ever extend to the earliest stages of information processing in the visual system (Finke 1980). For example, are neural units in the *retina* ever activated when a person forms a mental image? If this were the case, the visual characteristics of images would be *completely* equivalent to those of visually seen objects, since perception itself begins with stimulation of the retina. To determine the extent to which the principle of perceptual equivalence applies, one therefore needs to estab-

lish the most primitive levels of the visual system that are being used when images are formed.

An effective strategy for doing so is to see whether certain kinds of perceptual *aftereffects* ever result when appropriate patterns are visualized. Whenever neural mechanisms are activated for prolonged periods, they become fatigued and need time to recover. Because these units are often connected in a balanced way, the effects of neural fatigue create a temporary imbalance in the neural connections, resulting in distortions of normal perception. These distortions usually persist until the sensitivity of the fatigued units is restored. Finding that perceptual aftereffects can also occur following prolonged visualization of a stimulus would provide very strong evidence that these same neural mechanisms are being activated in imagery.

Consider, again, the question of whether mental images occur in the retina. One type of aftereffect, called a *color afterimage*, occurs whenever retinal photoreceptors have become fatigued. These afterimages appear as faint colors of opposite, or complementary, hue and can persist for several minutes. For example, if you stare at a red circle for a while, being careful to keep your gaze fixed, and then look at a sheet of white paper, you will notice a faint, green afterimage of the circle. The retinal photoreceptors (called "cones") are connected in such a way that complementary hues are in balance, with green being the complement to red. So a "negative," green afterimage results when a red pattern is observed, and vice versa. Now, suppose a person merely *imagined* looking at a red circle. Would he or she then "see" a green afterimage? If the principle of perceptual equivalence extends down to the retina, this should indeed happen.

Some early studies have reported that negative color afterimages sometimes do follow the visualization of colored objects under hypnosis (Erickson and Erickson 1938). The problem with these reports, however, is that the people who claim to have seen the negative color afterimages also tend to be the ones who already know about the afterimages (Barber 1964). Reports of negative color afterimages following visualization may therefore be due to the demand characteristics of the experiment, or to tacit knowledge, and not to an actual fatiguing of retinal photoreceptors.

2.3.3 *Imagery-Induced Color Aftereffects*
To get around this problem, Marty Schmidt and I made use of a striking but little-known aftereffect called the McCollough effect, named after Celeste McCollough (1965), who first reported it. The effect is produced by observing, in alternation, colored bar gratings

of opposite hue and orientation. For example, one might observe a horizontal, red and black grating alternating with a vertical, green and black grating. After several minutes of observing these patterns, one then sees negative color afterimages when looking at black and white gratings. The remarkable thing about these afterimages is that they are orientation-specific; for instance, a faint green hue would then be seen on a horizontal grating and a faint red hue on a vertical grating. The color afterimages would then be reversed by simply rotating the gratings by 90 degrees. They also last a surprisingly long time; unlike normal color afterimages, which fade after a minute or two, the McCollough effect can persist for days or even weeks (Jones and Holding 1975).

Schmidt and I wanted to find out whether the McCollough effect could be produced if the adaptation colors or gratings were generated in imagination (Finke and Schmidt 1977). We used two imagery conditions, one in which the subjects were instructed to visualize the colors red and green when shown an alternating sequence of horizontal and vertical achromatic gratings, and another in which they were instructed to visualize the bar gratings when shown an alternating sequence of featureless red and green color fields. These procedures were designed to simulate, using imagery to replace actual colors or bar gratings, the adaptation conditions that produce the McCollough effect. Because the afterimage colors in the McCollough effect are much weaker than those in normal color afterimages, we used a sensitive forced-choice testing procedure: the subjects were shown test patterns containing both horizontal and vertical achromatic gratings and were instructed to choose the grating that appeared "more red." The presence of a McCollough effect was then assessed by measuring the proportion of responses in which the association of color and orientation was opposite that during the adaptation procedure. To evaluate possible sources of response bias, the subjects were instructed at the end of the testing procedure to report any strategies they might have used to make their decisions.

We made the following predictions. First, if imagery can stimulate bar detectors and spatial frequency analyzers, as suggested by the studies on image acuity and probe detection, it should be possible to obtain the McCollough effect when bar gratings are imagined onto actual fields of color. Second, if imagery does not extend down to levels of the visual system where color afterimages are produced, then the McCollough effect should not appear when colors are imagined onto actual bar gratings. Third, because the McCollough effect is so unusual, subjects should not be able to guess what ought to happen, nor would they have tacit knowledge of the effect.

Initially, the subjects' reports indicated a strong response bias in the *opposite* direction to the McCollough effect: roughly half of them reported that they had perceived the task as a test of their "memory" for the pairing of color and orientation during the adaptation phase, and thus had chosen the gratings in the test patterns according to these remembered associations. The remainder of the subjects reported either irrelevant strategies or that they simply responded according to colors they actually saw on the test gratings; none reported deliberately associating color afterimages with orientation. The results for these subjects are presented in figure 2.9, along with the results of a perception condition, in which actual colored gratings were observed during the adaptation procedure. As this figure shows, there was evidence for a weak McCollough effect when bar gratings were imagined, but not when colors were imagined. This finding was replicated in a follow-up study with Schmidt, which controlled for the direction of scanning eye movements when subjects formed their images (Finke and Schmidt 1978).

2.3.4 Failures to Demonstrate Adaptation of Feature Detectors in Imagery
Were the orientation-specific color afterimages obtained in the Finke and Schmidt studies really the same as the McCollough effect? Ad-

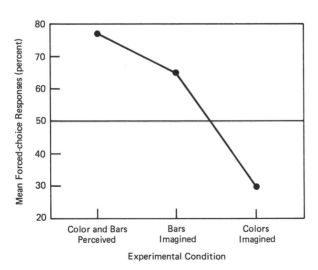

Figure 2.9
Mean proportion of responses indicating the presence of the McCollough effect, relative to chance level, when colored adaptation gratings were actually perceived, when bars were imagined and colors were perceived, and when colors were imagined and bars were perceived. The results suggest that orientation-specific color aftereffects can result when gratings, but not colors, are imagined. (from Finke and Schmidt 1977)

ditional studies have suggested that they probably are not. First, the imagery color aftereffects have not been obtained with other types of testing procedures that do reveal the actual McCollough effect; for example, having the subjects give magnitude estimates for the intensity of the color afterimages (see Broerse and Crassini 1980, 1984; Finke 1981). Also, there are a number of differences between the imagery color aftereffects and the McCollough effect. For instance, the imagery aftereffects are determined by the orientation of salient, local features in the adaptation patterns, whereas the actual McCollough effect is determined by the orientation of global features averaged across the adaptation patterns (Kunen and May 1980). In addition, the imagery aftereffects transfer interocularly, in contrast to the actual McCollough effect (Kaufman, May, and Kunen 1981). These differences call into question whether mental imagery really does involve the direct stimulation of bar detectors and other types of feature analyzers, as had been supposed. Instead, it seems more likely that the imagery-induced aftereffects are due to associations among visual features occurring at some higher level of the visual system.

A definitive study by Rhodes and O'Leary (1985) has recently shown that mental imagery does not produce the selective adaptation of bar or grating detectors in the human visual system. They had subjects visualize horizontal or vertical bar gratings continually for several minutes, and then measured changes in sensitivity for detecting actual gratings that were presented at low contrast. The orientation difference between the imagined and presented gratings had no effect on detection threshold. However, even a faint grating that was actually observed during the adaptation period produced an orientation-selective deficit in sensitivity. If bar or grating detectors had been activated during imagery, there should have been some evidence for a selective change in sensitivity, but there was none.

The conclusion follows that imagery and perception are not equivalent at levels of the visual system where the detection and analysis of elementary features take place. The correspondences between imagery and visual perception reviewed earlier in this chapter must therefore be imposed at some higher level of visual processing; at least, they cannot be attributed to the operating characteristics of orientation-specific feature detectors in the visual cortex. Apparently, these equivalences have more to do with the way visual features are associated than with the adaptation of feature analyzers, and the principle of perceptual equivalence must be restricted accordingly.

2.3.5 Imagery-Induced Prism Adaptation

In another series of experiments, I explored whether imagery could induce adaptation of the visual-motor system to optical distortions in vision. If one tries to point at an object while looking through prisms that cause the apparent locations of objects to be displaced, one will at first make errors to one side of the object but will then quickly adjust to the apparent displacement following repeated pointing attempts (see Harris 1965; Held 1965; Kohler 1962; Welch 1978). When the prisms are then removed, pointing aftereffects occur, that is, errors in the opposite direction, reflecting adjustments in visual-motor coordination that were made during the adaptation procedure. If the errors are observed only after the pointing attempts are completed, the pointing aftereffects transfer partially to the hand that was not used to point at the target object (Cohen 1967). Whereas the imagery aftereffects found with color-feature associations were relatively weak, and differed in various ways from those obtained using real adaptation gratings, pointing aftereffects occurring when errors of movement are imagined are very robust and correspond closely to those resulting when the errors are actually observed.

In one study (Finke 1979a), a group of subjects first participated in a perception condition, in which they pointed at a target that was visually displaced by the prisms and could see the errors they made. The rate at which their errors were reduced after twenty trials was recorded, and this was used to simulate prism adaptation in a second group of subjects. These subjects never saw their errors but merely imagined that they could see their pointing finger off to one side of the target, at the same locations where subjects in the perception condition had actually pointed. A set of markers was used to designate the sequence of these error locations. Subjects in a control condition pointed at the same prism-displaced target without seeing or imagining their errors. For all groups, pointing aftereffects were assessed for both the adapted and unadapted hands.

Figure 2.10 presents the rates of error reduction during the adaptation procedures in the three conditions. The adaptation rates were similar in imagery and perception, and both differed significantly from that in the control condition. The pointing aftereffects are shown in figure 2.11. Although the aftereffects in the perception condition were larger, overall, than those in the imagery condition, the imagery aftereffects were robust (shown by 85 percent of the subjects), and exhibited a similar, partial transfer to the unadapted hand. In addition, the imagery aftereffects were larger for subjects who rated their imagery as more vivid. There were no significant pointing aftereffects in the control condition.

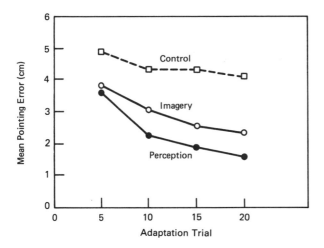

Figure 2.10
Mean rate of error reduction across prism adaptation trials, when subjects could see their errors, when they merely imagined their errors, and when they neither saw nor imagined their errors. The similar rates of error reduction in the perception and imagery conditions suggest that imagined errors of movement, like errors that are actually perceived, can lead to adaptive changes in visual-motor coordination. (from Finke 1979a)

These pointing aftereffects cannot easily be explained in terms of tacit knowledge, because prism adaptation is highly specialized and would seldom, if ever, be encountered in a natural environment. Almost certainly, one would never have had the opportunity to acquire tacit knowledge about the particular way prism-induced aftereffects transfer intermanually. Could these effects be due to experimenter bias or to the demand characteristics of the imagery task? This is also unlikely, in light of the results of a further experiment in the same study, which isolated the imagined errors from expectations for where the errors would actually be made. In this experiment the imagery condition of the first experiment was repeated, using two sets of error markers on opposite sides of the target. During the adaptation procedure, the subjects were instructed to imagine seeing their pointing finger arrive at the error markers on one side of the target, *but were led to believe that they would actually be making errors at the corresponding markers on the other side.* As before, it was emphasized that they should try to point as accurately as possible. In this case, the pointing shifts during the adaptation procedure, and the resulting aftereffects were determined by where the errors had been imagined, not by where they had been expected. This argues against any ac-

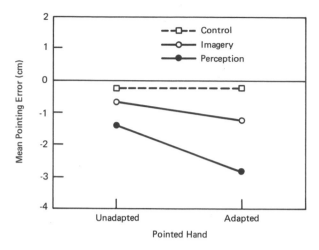

Figure 2.11
Mean pointing aftereffects following the prism adaptation conditions in figure 2.10, for the adapted and unadapted hands. The similar types of pointing aftereffects and intermanual transfer in the imagery and perception conditions suggest that imagined errors of movement can have residual effects on visual-motor coordination that correspond to those resulting from having actually perceived the errors. (from Finke 1979a)

count based on task demands for "correct" performance. Additional control experiments have since ruled out eye movements to the error markers as a possible explanation for the imagery-induced aftereffects (Finke 1979b).

Mental images for errors of movement thus appear to be functionally equivalent to actual, perceived errors in bringing about adaptive changes in visual-motor coordination. The principle of perceptual equivalence can therefore be extended to include visual mechanisms that are responsible for interpreting the consequences of erroneous bodily movements. Also, because these aftereffects are measured *after* the inducing stimulus is no longer imagined, they avoid problems (such as those considered in section 2.2) that could result when one tries to maintain an image while simultaneously judging its properties.

2.4 Image Facilitation of Perceptual Processes

Knowing that certain levels of the visual system are being stimulated during imagery does not in itself permit one to predict the effects of imagery on *ongoing* perceptual processes. For example, if you formed an image of an object just before the object was presented, how would your image influence your ability to perceive the object? Would it help or get in the way? Whether imagery facilitates or hinders perceptual processes is an empirical question that goes beyond whether or not imagery has genuine visual characteristics (Farah 1985; Finke, unpublished).

2.4.1 The Perceptual Anticipation Hypothesis

One possibility is that imagery would facilitate perception by "priming" mechanisms in the visual system, preparing them to receive information about a particular object or event (Beller 1971; Posner 1978). In other words, imagining an object would speed up perception by initiating the appropriate perceptual processes in advance. Ulric Neisser (1976) has proposed that images generally function as perceptual "anticipations" of this sort and become noticed by a person only when those expectations go unfulfilled. The perceptual anticipation hypothesis leads one to predict that forming a mental image of an object ought to make it easier to detect the object whenever the image and the object correspond (see also Cooper 1976a; Shepard 1978b).

2.4.2 Detecting Letters While Imagining Them

Martha Farah (1985) has recently carried out experiments showing that, by imagining letters of the alphabet that match presented letters, one can increase one's ability to detect the letters. Her subjects were shown the letters H or T after being instructed to form a mental image of one of them. The letters were presented at low contrast in one of two consecutive observation intervals, and the subjects' task was to report the interval in which either of the target letters appeared. This method was used because it avoids the problem of response bias to the target letter. In addition to varying whether the presented and imagined letters had the same shape, Farah also varied whether the letters were imagined in the same location where they were presented. A control condition was included, in which the detection task was performed without imagery instructions. The subjects were more accurate in detecting the presented letters, relative to the control condition, when the images matched the targets in both shape and location. However, when the images did not match the targets, or differed in location, detection was less accurate than in the control condition. More recently, Farah (in press) has shown that the way imagery facilitates perception in this task resembles the way selective attention to the presented letters improves their detection. These findings support the perceptual anticipation hypothesis, suggesting that mental imagery functions to selectively prime visual pathways that will be used in detecting an object.

2.4.3 The Effects of Imagining a Visual Context

Another way in which imagery might facilitate perception is by providing a visual context in which the relevant perceptual processes can be carried out more efficiently. For example, Peterson and Graham (1974) found that subjects were able to detect pictures of common objects (such as a spoon) more accurately after visualizing scenes in which the objects would naturally appear ("a spoon on the floor with ants on it"). In contrast, detection of the objects was impaired whenever the imagined scenes were incompatible with them.

In the Peterson and Graham study the effects of imagining the context scenes might have been due to the subjects' expectations of seeing the particular objects that the scenes contained. This is a potential problem, in fact, in any study in which the imagined objects can also *be* one of the targets. What one needs to do is to demonstrate that imagined contexts can facilitate perception when the context neither contains nor suggests any of the potential targets.

Jennifer Freyd and I reported one type of image facilitation that meets this criterion (Freyd and Finke 1984a). Subjects were presented with cross-shaped patterns consisting of a vertical line bisected by a horizontal line that was slightly different in length, and their task was to say which of the two lines was longer. On half the trials they were to imagine a context pattern before the lines appeared, consisting of either an outlined square or an X centered over the two lines (see figure 2.12). The sides of the square were slightly shorter than either of the lines, which we expected would facilitate the length discriminations, whereas the "X" pattern was expected to have little or no effect. Because these context patterns were symmetrical with respect to the target lines, they would not bias subjects

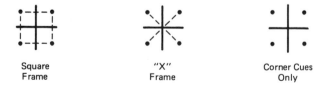

Square   "X"   Corner Cues
Frame   Frame   Only

Figure 2.12
Context patterns that subjects were to imagine in experiments on visual discrimination. On imagery trials, the subjects were to judge whether the horizontal or vertical line was longer after mentally superimposing one of the context patterns over them. On baseline trials, corner cues for the context patterns were not presented. (from Freyd and Finke 1984a)

to select one response over the other. The corners of each of the context patterns were designated in advance by small dots that were removed just before the target lines appeared. The discrimination times were compared with those in a baseline condition, in which the corner cues were not presented, with those in a control condition, in which the corner cues were presented without imagery instructions, and with those in a perception condition, in which the context patterns were actually presented. As shown in figure 2.13, the discrimination times were fastest when the subjects had imagined or observed the square context pattern in advance. In contrast, there was no significant effect on the discrimination times from having imagined or observed the X pattern. When the corner cues had been presented without imagery instructions, subjects reported that they often imagined the square frame spontaneously; in this case there was an intermediate degree of facilitation. The imagined contexts were thus equivalent to the perceived contexts in their effects on the length discriminations.

Other studies have shown that *errors* in making length discriminations can be induced when the imagined contexts correspond to those used in standard visual illusions. For example, in an experiment by Benjamin Wallace (1984), subjects were instructed to visu-

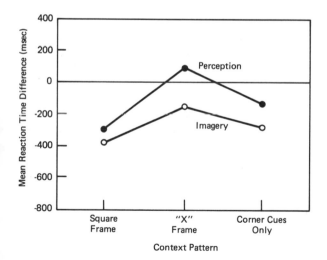

Figure 2.13
Mean reaction time difference, with respect to baseline performance, for having perceived or imagined context patterns prior to making the length discriminations of figure 2.12. The correspondence between the functions suggests that appropriately imagined contexts, like perceived contexts, can facilitate performance on discrimination tasks. (from Freyd and Finke 1984a)

alize an inverted V over a pair of horizontal lines, in such a manner as to simulate the Ponzo illusion (see Coren and Girgus 1978). An illustration of the Ponzo illusion is shown in figure 2.14; the top line appears longer than the bottom line, even though the two lines are identical in length. Subjects who were able to mentally superimpose the context pattern over the lines all reported, erroneously, that the top line appeared longer, and their estimates for the difference in the lengths of the lines were equivalent to those when the context pattern was actually shown surrounding the lines. The use of a naive experimenter in this study minimized the possibility that the subjects' performance could have been due to experimenter bias (cf. Singer and Sheehan 1965).

These findings on the effects of imagining visual contexts provide further support for the idea that imagery and perception are equivalent down to levels of the visual system where simple features are associated. In addition, they show that the interaction of perceived and imagined features can sometimes result in improved perception and sometimes in erroneous perception, depending on the nature of these associations.

2.4.4 The Problem of Eye Movements
One factor that was not systematically controlled in any of the studies considered in the previous section was the possible effects of eye movements when the images were formed. For example, subjects in the Freyd and Finke study might have looked at different parts of the target pattern depending on the type of context pattern they were imagining, and this might have influenced their reaction times. In the Wallace study, subjects might have looked at the two parallel lines differently when imagining the surrounding patterns, resulting in changes in the apparent lengths of the lines. In general, eye movements can be a potential problem whenever a presented pattern

Figure 2.14
Example of the Ponzo illusion. The surrounding context pattern makes the top horizontal line appear longer, even though the two lines are actually the same length. This and similar illusions were created by instructing subjects to imagine the context pattern. (from Wallace 1984)

is judged in conjunction with an imagined pattern (Farah, in press; Finke 1985). Whether these and the results of other experiments on interactions between imagery and perception can actually be accounted for in terms of eye movements remains to be seen. It should be noted, however, that Farah and Smith (1983) have found that imagined auditory *tones* can facilitate the detection of presented matching tones, in which case the issue of eye movements is irrelevant.

2.5 Interference Between Imagery and Perception

Complicating the perceptual anticipation hypothesis are findings showing that an imagined stimulus that corresponds more closely to a presented stimulus can sometimes selectively *interfere* with perception.

2.5.1 The Perky Effect
An early study by Perky (1910) reported a curious phenomenon. When subjects were told to imagine looking at an object (such as a "banana") on a supposedly blank screen, while actually being shown a faint picture of the object, they sometimes confused the picture with their image. The reason, according to Perky, was that an image was phenomenally similar to a faint visual stimulus. Although this study did not include modern controls for experimenter effects and the like, it at least raises the question of whether imagery could also interfere with perception when the two correspond, instead of facilitating it. Recall, by way of comparison, the experiments on reality monitoring considered in section 1.4.5, in which subjects often confused memories for similar imagined and perceived events.

2.5.2 Reduction in Detection Sensitivity During Imagination
Evidence that visual imagery can impair visual perception, as opposed to other forms of imagery that are not visual, was reported by Segal and Fusella (1970). Subjects were presented with faint geometric forms or auditory tones as target stimuli, while imagining other objects or sounds. Using the bias-free methods of *signal detection* (Green and Swets 1966), Segal and Fusella found that perceptual sensitivity was maximally reduced when the modality of the image matched that of the target. For instance, it was harder to detect a faint geometric form when imagining a visual scene than when imagining a familiar sound. In a sense, this is the Brooks interference finding in reverse (see section 1.3.2), which had shown that visualization is selectively impaired during perception.

One needs to consider, again, whether eye movements during visualization might have been responsible for these findings. In fact, there is a particular form of the eye movement criticism that applies specifically to these types of studies: it is possible that visual imagery could influence visual sensitivity indirectly, by inducing changes in pupil diameter or accommodation (Bower 1972; Malmstrom and Randle 1976). This criticism was addressed by Reeves and Segal (1973). They replicated the results of Segal and Fusella but found no consistent relationship between the effects of imagery and measured changes in pupil diameter or eye position.

2.5.3 Comparing Visual Identification and Detection

The contrasting findings on image facilitation and interference seem paradoxical. On the one hand, imagery can improve perception; on the other hand, it sometimes impairs perception. It is difficult to pinpoint the precise reasons for these differing results, because the studies used different types of stimuli and procedures and also differed in the extent to which the images matched the presented stimuli. I have tried to sort out some of these factors by comparing the effects of image formation and image-target alignment in two different types of tasks.

In an experiment on visual identification, subjects had to say on each trial whether a horizontal or vertical bar had been presented (Finke 1986b). The bars could be easily discriminated, and the subjects' reaction times were recorded. On most of the trials, the subjects were instructed to visualize a bar, in advance, that was horizontal, vertical, or at some orientation in between; in this way the alignment between the imagined and presented bars was systematically varied (see figure 2.15). To minimize the effects of expectations, the subjects were explicitly told that there would be no relation between the type of image formed and the likelihood of being presented with a particular target bar. In comparison with their performance on control trials, where they were told not to form an image, it took the subjects less time to identify the bars when the imagined and presented bars were perfectly aligned, but more time when the imagined bars were oriented in between the target bar orientations (see figure 2.16).

In a corresponding experiment on visual detection, the subjects merely reported whether either of the two bars had been presented, without having to identify them. In this case, reaction time *increased* as the imagined and presented bars became more closely aligned, in contrast with the results for the identification task (see again figure 2.16). Thus, whether imagery facilitates or interferes with performance on a perceptual task depends not only on whether the image

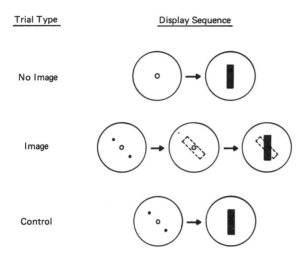

Figure 2.15
Examples of display sequences used in experiments on visual identification and detection. The subjects were to identify vertical and horizontal target bars or merely to
detect their presence. On imagery trials, they were to imagine a bar aligned with the
orientation cues prior to the onset of the target bar. This provided a method for
varying the alignment between the imagined bar and the target. On control trials, the
orientation cues were presented without imagery instructions, and on baseline trials
the orientation cues were not presented. (from Finke 1986b)

matches the target but also on the nature of the task (see also Over
and Broerse 1972; Reeves 1980). These contrasting findings are not
easily explained in terms of shifts in eye position that might have
occurred with changing orientations of the imagined bars; this would
have produced similar effects of image alignment in the two experiments. Again, it is not sufficient to know only that imagery and
perception share many of the same visual characteristics when trying
to understand how imagery influences perception.

2.6 Summary and Conclusions

Mental images have many visual characteristics in common with
perceived objects and events. They exhibit constraints on resolution
that, in many respects, correspond to those in visual perception.
They can lead to changes in visual-motor coordination that resemble
those resulting when one adapts to actual visual distortions. And
they can provide visual contexts that influence perception in much
the same way as actual visual contexts. The principle of perceptual
equivalence is supported by these findings, but there are limitations

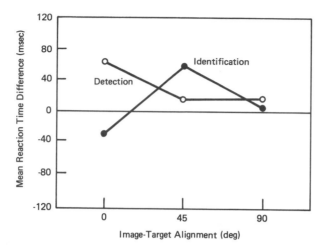

Figure 2.16
Mean reaction time difference, with respect to baseline performance, for having imagined a bar prior to the onset of a target bar in identification and detection tasks, as
the alignment between the imagined and target bars varied. The contrasting results
suggest that, when an image matches a target, though it can help one to identify the
target, it can also interfere with detecting the target. (from Finke 1986b)

on how far down in the visual system the principle applies. Mental
imagery does not seem to involve retinal or precortical levels of the
visual system, which are primarily responsible for chromatic aftereffects. Nor does it seem likely that imagery involves the initial stages
of information processing in the visual cortex, where simple feature
analysis takes place. Rather, the principle appears to hold only down
to levels in the visual system where visual associations occur. The
principle is also limited with respect to how mental images would
influence ongoing perceptual processes. Whether imagery facilitates
or interferes with performance on perceptual tasks appears to be a
complex issue, one that cannot be resolved simply from knowing the
visual properties of an image.

2.7 Further Explorations

2.7.1 Recommendations for Further Reading
Additional discussion of experiments relating imagery to perception
can be found in articles by Finke (1980, 1985, 1986a), Finke and
Shepard (1986), and Shepard and Podgorny (1978). Articles by Banks
(1981) and by Intons-Peterson and White (1981) have criticized many
of these experiments.

2.7.2 Estimating the Physical Attributes of Real and Imagined Objects
Imagery and perception have also been compared using the psycho-physical technique of *magnitude estimation*, in which one employs a numerical scale to rate a stimulus along some dimension, such as size. Typically, these estimates are related to the actual values of a stimulus by power functions, and the exponents of the functions indicate the degree to which the range of judged values is compressed or expanded relative to the actual stimulus values. Using this technique, Kerst and Howard (1978) obtained magnitude estimates of the distances between the centers of U.S. states and the areas of the states, while subjects looked at a map, or recalled the map from memory. The exponents for the power functions for distance and area estimates were 1.04 and .79, respectively, in the perception condition, and 1.10 and .60, respectively, in the memory condition. The exponents in the memory condition were thus approximately equal to the *square* of the corresponding exponents in the perception condition. This finding was replicated and extended by Moyer et al. (1978).

Kerst and Howard proposed the following explanation for this relationship between the exponents. In the memory condition, the subjects had formed mental images of the states and thus, in effect, were "reperceiving" them. This is why the exponents in the memory condition were roughly equal to the square of those in the perception condition. Whatever kind of scaling transformation is imposed during the initial act of perceiving an object would then be imposed once again when the object is visualized. Although appealing, this explanation runs into difficulties. It suggests, for example, that objects should always be remembered as smaller than they actually are, and this does not seem to be true. Also, the results of Finke and Kurtzman (1981a) suggest that the areas of patterns are remembered accurately when subjects are given an adequate opportunity to study the patterns. This strong version of the "reperceptual" hypothesis is thus in need of further confirmation.

2.7.3 "Point of View" in Remembering Details of Stories
The visual field in imagery may play a role in determining the kinds of details that people remember when they read a story. Fiske et al. (1979) asked subjects to identify with a particular character in stories they were reading, and their memory for incidental details mentioned in the stories was then tested. Fiske et al. found that the details that the subjects were able to recall tended to be those that the character they had identified with would have been able to "see," from his or

her viewing perspective in the story. This suggests that visual imagery may lead to better memory for information that is mentioned or implied in verbal descriptions, whenever that information can be included within the imagery field (see also the relevant discussions of the *implicit encoding* principle in chapter 1).

Chapter 3

Spatial Characteristics of Mental Images

Whereas chapter 2 concentrated mainly on the visual characteristics of images, this chapter will be devoted to studies that have examined the general, spatial characteristics of images. These studies, too, bear directly on the issue of whether the properties of images can be explained solely in terms of conscious, guessing strategies, or tacit, propositional relationships that underlie the formation of an image. We begin by considering a third imagery principle.

3.1 The Principle of Spatial Equivalence

Many of the studies reviewed in the first two chapters suggest that mental images have a spatial "extent." For example, experiments on using images to verify the presence of parts of objects, which were discussed in section 1.6, suggest that images have a definite "size." Experiments on measuring the imagery field, discussed in section 2.1, reveal that images can "overflow" if they become too large. Studies on imagery mnemonics, discussed in section 1.4, suggest that one can imagine the locations of objects along a route. Our third principle, the principle of *spatial equivalence*, pertains to the faithfulness with which spatial relations among objects and their parts are preserved in an image:

The spatial arrangement of the elements of a mental image corresponds to the way objects or their parts are arranged on actual physical surfaces or in an actual physical space.

This principle requires that mental images, like a physical surface or space, be spatially *continuous*. This means that relative distances must actually be depicted in an image, rather than being displayed in a propositional or some listlike fashion. Also, between any two points on an imagined surface, or within an imagined space, all intermediate points must be depicted as well, just as on an actual, continuous physical surface or within a physical space. We will assume in this chapter that the imagery "medium" corresponds to a

Euclidian surface or space, although the principle need not be restricted to such cases.

Note that the principle of spatial equivalence goes beyond what is implied by the principle of perceptual equivalence, which was considered in chapter 2. Mental images need not exhibit *visual* characteristics per se (such as limits on resolution, visual aftereffects, etc.) in order that they preserve *spatial* relations among objects. You can perceive that something has a spatial extent, for example, without necessarily looking at it.

The person who is most closely identified with this principle is Stephen Kosslyn, whose work on imagery has already been mentioned in previous chapters. Kosslyn and his colleagues have conducted numerous studies on the spatial properties of mental images, using the technique of instructing subjects to scan their images from one imagined location to another. The time it takes the subjects to complete the imagined scanning reveals information about the way locations and distances are represented in images. Kosslyn's experiments and their implications will be considered in the remainder of this section.

3.1.1 The Imagined Scanning of Pictures and Maps

In Kosslyn (1973), subjects learned drawings of familiar objects that were elongated horizontally or vertically, such as those shown in figure 3.1. Each of the drawings contained three prominent parts, located at the top (or right side), the middle, and the bottom (or left side). For example, the drawing of a tower contained a door at the

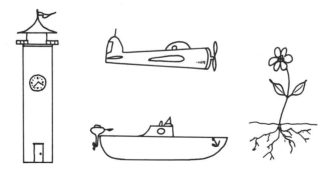

Figure 3.1
Examples of drawings used in experiments on imagined scanning. The subjects were instructed to mentally focus on one end of the drawing, and then to "look" for a designated feature of the drawing on their image. The time it took them to do so increased as the distance between the feature and the initial point of focus increased. (from Kosslyn 1973)

bottom, a clock in the middle, and a flag at the top. The trials began by playing a tape recording of the name of the drawing, followed by the name of a part. In one condition, the subjects were instructed to form an image of the whole drawing and then "look for" the designated part on their image. In another condition, they were told to focus on a specific end of the drawing (top, bottom, right, or left) as soon as they had formed their image. The measure of interest was reaction time for verifying that the named part was present in the drawing.

Kosslyn reasoned that if spatial relations among parts of an object are preserved in a mental image, it should take longer to find the named part when one starts out by mentally focusing on the wrong end of the drawing. In other words, just as it takes longer to scan between two points that are farther apart on an actual drawing, so, too, should it take longer to imagine scanning between the same two points on a mental image. Kosslyn's results confirmed this prediction: when the subjects had imagined focusing on the ends of the drawings, the time it took them to verify that the named parts belonged to the object increased as the parts were farther removed from the point of focus. In contrast, when they had not imagined focusing on the ends of the drawings, their verification times did not depend on where the parts were located.

There are, however, other explanations for these findings that don't rely on the assumption that images preserve spatial relations. Using the method of loci, which was described in section 1.4.4, Lea (1975) found that the number of items scanned over, as opposed to the actual scanning distance, could have been responsible for Kosslyn's results. Lea's subjects were instructed to memorize a layout of 12 objects located at various positions along a circular path, and then to associate target items to each of these objects. For example, if the object was a "bicycle" and the target item a "policeman," they were to imagine that the policeman was standing next to the bicycle. They were then given one of the objects as a cue and were instructed to mentally focus on the location of that object and to report other objects or target items that were a certain number of positions away along the path. Their task therefore consisted of three operations: finding the starting locus, mentally moving from locus to locus while keeping track of the number of loci scanned, and retrieving the object or target item at the final position. Lea found that the reaction times for completing the task increased in proportion to the number of loci that had to be scanned, but were not affected by changes in the separation distance for a given number of loci. Because these two factors, distance and the number of items scanned, had been confounded in Kosslyn's study, Lea concluded that images might not preserve the spatial characteristics of physical objects.

On the contrary, these results are more consistent with the predictions of propositional models (see section 1.5.5), which would assume that the underlying representations depict ordinal, as opposed to spatial, relations. For example, a propositional model would typically represent objects as nodes in a semantic network, and their relationships in terms of associative links connecting the nodes (Anderson 1976). Mentally scanning over consecutive objects in this type of representation would consist of moving consecutively from one node to another along these connective links. Only the ordinal relations among objects would be an inherent property of this kind of representation; in this respect the representation would resemble a list rather than a picture or spatial array.

Kosslyn, Ball, and Reiser (1978) conducted additional experiments on image scanning to address the problems raised by Lea. They pointed out that in Lea's study, subjects were never given explicit instructions to *scan* images of the mental paths. If it were more efficient to use listlike or propositional representations to retrieve the needed information, rather than to scan mental images, Lea's failure to find an effect of separation distance would not be surprising. For this reason, Kosslyn et al. explored the effects of varying both the interobject separation distance and the number of intervening items when subjects were explicitly told to scan their mental images.

In their first experiment, subjects memorized the locations of three letters positioned along a straight line. They were then instructed to imagine focusing on one end of the line, and to imagine scanning along the line to indicate whether a designated letter was upper or lower in case. The target letter was at one of three equally spaced distances from the point of focus and was separated by 0, 1, or 2 intervening letters. The reaction time for correctly identifying the case of the target letters increased, independently, with scanning distance and the number of intervening letters. In other words, scanning distance and the number of intervening items had additive effects on reaction time. The additive effect of the number of intervening items reflected, presumably, the additional time required to mentally "inspect" each of the items before reaching the target letter. Kosslyn et al. noted that scanning distance influenced the response times even when there were *no* intervening items, which would argue against any account based on recalling an ordered sequence of items.

In this experiment, only three scanning distances were used. To find out whether mental images preserve spatial information across a wide range of distances, Kosslyn et al. conducted a second experiment, the now-classic "map-scanning" experiment. Subjects learned the locations of seven objects on a fictional map, shown in figure 3.2. The objects were positioned to create 21 scanning distances ranging from 2 to 19 cm, with no intervening objects along any of the scan paths. The subjects were instructed to mentally focus on an object when it was named, and then to imagine scanning to a second object to verify that it was also on the map. The imagined scanning was to be performed by imagining a small black "speck" moving across the map in a direct, straight-line path from the first object to the second. Reaction times for correctly verifying the presence of the second object were recorded for all possible object pairs. The results, presented in figure 3.3, show a striking linear correspondence between interobject distance and reaction time. In a control experiment, in which the subjects were not explicitly instructed to imagine scanning the map, there was no relationship between response time and interobject distance. These findings, then, suggest that mental images do preserve spatial relations, at least along flat, two-dimensional surfaces.

3.1.2 The Imagined Scanning of Three-Dimensional Arrays

One might also consider whether it is possible to imagine scanning a set of objects in depth. If mental images preserve only two-dimen-

Figure 3.2
Fictional map that subjects imagined scanning. The objects on the map were positioned to create 21 unique scanning distances. (from Kosslyn, Ball, and Reiser 1978)

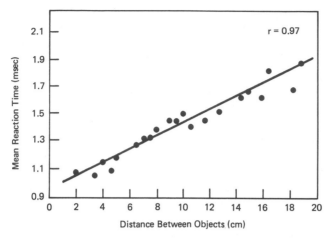

Figure 3.3
Mean reaction time to imagine scanning between pairs of objects on the fictional map shown in figure 3.2, as the distance between the objects increased. The linear increase in reaction time with increasing scanning distance suggests that images can preserve the two-dimensional distances on actual maps. (from Kosslyn, Ball, and Reiser 1978)

sional distances, for example, the imagined scanning of a three-dimensional array of objects would merely resemble the scanning of flat, viewer-centered representations of the objects, such as a photograph. Knowing whether people can imagine scanning objects in three dimensions would further reveal the extent to which spatial relations are preserved in a mental image.

The imagined scanning of three-dimensional arrays has been investigated in a series of experiments by Steven Pinker (1980). At the beginning of his experiments, subjects learned the locations of five small toys suspended inside of an open box. These objects were positioned such that their three-dimensional separation distances would differ from their two-dimensional distances, as projected along a surface perpendicular to the observer's line of sight. In Pinker's first experiment, the subjects were instructed to close their eyes, to mentally focus on one of the objects, and then to imagine scanning directly along a straight line to a second, named object. As in the Kosslyn, Ball, and Reiser study, they were told to do this by imagining that a small black "speck" was moving rapidly from the first object to the second. Pinker found that the scanning times were highly correlated with the interobject distances in three-dimensional space, but not with the two-dimensional distances between projections of the objects, which would have resulted if images were simply flat, two-dimensional representations, like photographs. (See also section 1.5 for additional sources of evidence that images are not literally like photographs.) The linear reaction-time function for imagined scanning in depth is shown in figure 3.4.

Pinker then performed several clever variations of this experiment. He wanted to see whether people *could* imagine scanning along the two-dimensional, projected interobject distances if specifically instructed to do so. This time, the subjects were told to imagine that there was a glass plate covering the front opening of the box, and to imagine that they were moving a rifle sight along the surface of the glass plate from one object to another. In this case, their scanning times were highly correlated with the two-dimensional distances, but not with the three-dimensional distances. Pinker then instructed the subjects to repeat this "rifle scope" task while imagining that they were looking at the same array of objects from above or from the side. Their scanning times were now proportional to the two-dimensional distances as seen from the new vantage points.

Pinker was therefore able to show that people can imagine scanning objects either in depth or along flat, two-dimensional projections of the objects. This suggests that the principle of spatial equivalence

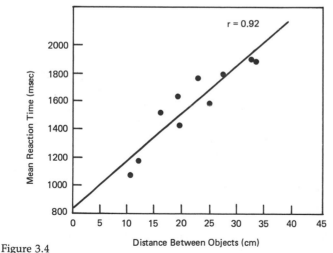

Figure 3.4

Mean reaction time to imagine scanning between pairs of objects in a three-dimensional array. The linear increase in reaction time with increasing scanning distance in depth suggests that images can also preserve three-dimensional distances. (from Pinker 1980)

applies to three-dimensional spaces as well as to flat surfaces. Control experiments, also conducted by Pinker, showed that these results could not be attributed to eye movements, which, as discussed in section 2.4.4, can be a potential problem in imagery experiments. When subjects were instructed to move their eyes from one object to another, their response times were much faster and were proportional only to the two-dimensional separation distances.

There is another variation of these experiments that deserves mention. Pinker and Kosslyn (1978) found that the reaction times for imagined scanning in depth were still proportional to the three-dimensional separation distances even after subjects were instructed to imagine moving one or more of the objects in the initial configuration. This suggests that images can preserve information about relative three-dimensional distances even after the imagined configurations are mentally rearranged. This is why, for example, people can often visualize what a room would look like after rearranging the furniture.

3.2 Criticisms of the Image-Scanning Experiments

There have been several recent criticisms of studies on image scanning that must be addressed in considering the principle of spatial equivalence.

3.2.1 Continuity of the Scanning Process

One question that remains is whether the imagined scanning is necessarily continuous. Perhaps, when subjects are instructed to imagine scanning from one point to another, what they actually do is erase their initial image, construct a totally new image, and then imagine focusing on the second point in their new image. If, for some reason, the time it takes to do this is proportional to the distance between the two points—for example, it might take longer to construct a second image centered on a point farther away—then the reaction times might resemble those obtained in image-scanning studies, but without there being any actual scanning of the images.

Kosslyn (1980) has shown that this so-called "blink transformation" of an image cannot account for the results of the previous studies. Subjects were instructed to imagine drawings of faces containing a mouth and either light or dark eyes, in which the distance between the mouth and the eyes was varied. They were to begin by imagining that they were looking at the mouth, and then, when the cue word "light" or "dark" was given, to verify whether the eyes corresponded to the cue. In one condition, they were specifically told to do this by erasing their first image, which was focused on the mouth, and forming a new image, which was focused on the eyes. Their verification times, in this case, were unrelated to the distance between the features. In contrast, when the subjects were told to imagine scanning to the eyes before responding, their verification times increased in the usual way with the distance separating the features (Kosslyn, Ball, and Reiser 1978). *These results imply that reaction time increases with distance only when subjects do in fact perform the imagined scanning.* Kosslyn (1980) has suggested that in lieu of specific instructions for how to locate features in an imagery task, either a "blink" or a "scan" process will be used, depending on which is more efficient.

3.2.2 The Tacit Knowledge Critique of Image Scanning

It still does not necessarily follow that the rates of imagined scanning reflect the inherent spatial properties of images. Zenon Pylyshyn (1981) has raised the provocative alternative that the results of image-scanning experiments are due instead to tacit knowledge that people possess about how physical distances are supposed to be scanned. The role that tacit knowledge might play in other kinds of imagery experiments was considered previously in section 2.2.5; it is particularly relevant to image-scanning experiments. According to Pylyshyn's critique, reaction time increases with distance not because imagery exists within a spatial medium, but because people tacitly know that longer physical distances take more time to scan. Hence, they adjust their response times accordingly. In Pylyshyn's terms, the scanning task is *cognitively penetrable*, meaning that the way the task is performed can depend on the subjects' beliefs and on the demands of the experiment.

Pylyshyn cites findings by Bannon (1981) in support of the tacit knowledge account. In Bannon's experiments, subjects learned the locations of features on a map and were instructed to visualize the map and to focus their attention on one of the features, as in the study of Kosslyn, Ball, and Reiser (1978). When the subjects were told to imagine scanning from the first feature to the second, their response times were highly correlated with distance, replicating the results of Kosslyn et al. However, when they were told simply to give the compass direction from the first feature to the second (north, southeast, etc.), their response times were not related to the distance between the features. A similar failure to obtain evidence for image scanning when subjects are asked to make directional judgments in imagery, but are not explicitly told to scan their images, was reported by Wilton (1979). Pylyshyn concluded, therefore, that the distance-time correlations in previous image-scanning studies are merely a consequence of tacit knowledge that subjects can draw on whenever they are instructed to mentally simulate the scanning of a physical array.

An analogy may help to clarify how tacit knowledge could conceivably "contaminate" an image-scanning experiment. Imagine placing a ball on a flat surface. Now suppose you wanted to move the ball to some other spot on the surface. There are two ways you could do this. First, you could push the ball in the right direction and let it roll toward the second spot. In this case, the time it would take the ball to arrive would be proportional to the distance between the points, assuming that the ball rolls at a constant rate of speed. This corresponds to an imagined scan. Second, you could simply lift the ball off the surface and then place it down on the second spot. Suppose, in this case, you wanted to *simulate* the rolling motion without actually letting the ball roll. You could do so by delaying when you put the ball down, according to your knowledge about distance-time relationships that govern the ball's actual motion. This corresponds to the way tacit knowledge might influence response times in an image-scanning experiment. Note that reaction time in the latter instance would depend *arbitrarily* on the extent of your knowledge about the motions to be simulated, whereas in the first instance it would depend *invariably* on the properties of the surface.

Tacit knowledge, in fact, may govern response times even if the imagined scanning is actually carried out. To extend the analogy, suppose you did roll the ball across the surface but controlled how quickly the ball moved, again according to your knowledge about the rate at which the motion should proceed. This implies that even when subjects claim they are carrying out an imagined scan, there is still the possibility that tacit knowledge might influence their response times.

Kosslyn (1981) points out that the tacit knowledge account is actually based on three assumptions: that the task itself suggests that one is supposed to perform a mental simulation of physical motion, that one possesses tacit knowledge of how the motion ought to proceed, and that one can successfully apply that knowledge to carry out the mental simulation. *All* of these conditions would have to be met; even then, the tacit knowledge account would have little explanatory power. If a person's tacit beliefs are unconstrained, so that they could be anything at all, then virtually any imagery finding could, in principle, be explained by them. (See the related discussion of this point in section 2.2.5.)

3.2.3 Task Demands in Image-Scanning Experiments

The reason the tacit knowledge account cannot be dismissed in the case of image scanning is that these experiments typically *do* create task demands for carrying out mental simulations of simple physical motions. Indeed, there is evidence that subjects can easily predict the relations between distance and scanning time that are obtained in many of these experiments, when encouraged to do so. For example, Mitchell and Richman (1980) had subjects learn the same map used by Kosslyn, Ball, and Reiser and asked them merely to guess how long it would take to imagine scanning from one object on the map to another. The estimated scanning times were highly correlated with the interobject distances, implying that subjects in actual image-scanning experiments could have used similar estimates to adjust their response times (see also Richman, Mitchell, and Reznick 1979).

This account, however, would have a harder time explaining the results of Pinker's (1980) study on the imagined scanning of three-dimensional arrays, which was described in section 3.1.2. Recall that Pinker's subjects could imagine scanning over two-dimensional projected distances that corresponded to how the arrays would look from *novel* viewing perspectives. These distances would not have been apparent from the original viewing perspective, and thus the obtained relations between distance and scanning time would have been difficult for the subjects to anticipate.

3.2.4 Experimenter Bias Revisited

Another possibility is that experimenter bias could have influenced subjects' performance in experiments on image scanning. As suggested by Intons-Peterson (1983), subjects may respond to subtle cues for correct performance communicated by experimenters who expect that the scanning times should be proportional to the scanning distances (see also section 2.2.4). Evidence that experimenter bias is not a crucial factor in these experiments comes from a study by Jolicoeur and Kosslyn (1985). The Kosslyn, Ball, and Reiser experiment on scanning imagined maps was again repeated, except that the experimenters were led to expect that the relation between reaction time and distance should resemble a U-shaped function, instead of a linear function. (The "justification" given for why reaction times would increase for short as well as long separation distances was that when objects on the imagined map were close together, they would be harder to distinguish.) Despite having these misleading expectations, the experimenters obtained (to their dismay) the usual linear increase in reaction time with increasing scanning distance. Likewise, the overall rate of imagined scanning was not affected by the experimenters' expectations for how quickly the scanning process should occur.

It is still possible, however, that subjects in these experiments are being influenced to some extent by the demands of the experimental task. Goldston, Hinrichs, and Richman (1985) have reported that correlations between distance and reaction time in image-scanning experiments, as well as the measured rates of scanning, are reduced when subjects are told to expect that their scanning times would decrease, rather than increase, with longer distances.

3.3 Extensions of the Scanning Paradigm

A lingering problem with most of these image-scanning studies is that the predicted relations between scanning distance and response time are much too obvious. Additional studies, employing different methods, have since been conducted to address this problem.

3.3.1 The Functional Value of Image Scanning

Because mental image scanning has so far been demonstrated only when subjects are explicitly told to imagine that they are scanning pictures or maps, image scanning may have no real "purpose," other than to provide a convenient experimental tool for measuring the spatial properties of an image. As we have seen, this invites the criticism that subjects might base their performance on what they know about how actual scanning occurs, in response to task demands that are created by the image-scanning instructions. Much stronger evidence that the scanning times reflect the inherent spatial characteristics of images would come from demonstrations that image scanning is sometimes used *spontaneously*, without one's having to be instructed to use it.

Pinker and I have undertaken a series of experiments to try to establish that image scanning does indeed have a useful function. We began by having subjects learn a configuration of dots that were randomly positioned on an otherwise blank screen (Finke and Pinker 1982). The dots were then presented individually to the subjects, along with an arrow that was pointing away from the dots. The subjects' task was to say whether or not the arrow was pointing to any of the other dots in the original configuration. We thought they might have to perform this task by imagining that they were scanning from one dot to another, along the direction designated by the arrow. However, in agreement with the findings of Bannon (1981) and Wilton (1979), described in section 3.2.2, we could find no evidence that reaction time increased with increasing distance separating the dots, suggesting that image scanning was not being used to perform the task.

It then became evident that in each of these studies the subjects would already have known the proper directions from one object to another, since they had initially learned the relative positions of the objects. There would then be no reason for them to carry out an imagined scan in order to judge these directions, unless they were specifically told to do so. Indeed, in all the previous studies on image scanning, subjects must already have known where one object was in relation to another, in order to initiate the imagined scan in the first place. This would explain why image scanning does not occur spontaneously under these conditions.

Suppose, however, that subjects did not have advance information about where one object was in relation to another, when having to judge their relative directions. They might then have to imagine scanning between the objects. In other words, image scanning might be used spontaneously whenever people need to verify spatial relations that were not explicitly encoded. The principle of implicit encoding, which was discussed in chapter 1, might therefore extend to the functional uses of mental image scanning.

To explore this possibility, Pinker and I modified the arrow-verification task in the following way. The subjects were shown a random dot pattern for a brief, five-second inspection period. After a one-second retention interval, they were then shown an arrow pointing from an *unexpected* location. An example of this presentation sequence is illustrated in figure 3.5. Their task was to indicate, as quickly as possible, whether the arrow was pointing at any of the previously seen dots. Even though mental imagery and image scanning were never mentioned, the subjects' response times increased linearly as the arrow-dot distance increased. The rate of increase was

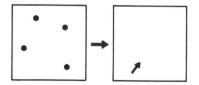

Figure 3.5
Example of a presentation sequence in experiments on the spontaneous use of mental image scanning (left). The subjects were to judge whether an arrow was pointing at any of the dots seen in the previous dot pattern. They reported doing the task by imagining that they were scanning along the direction specified by the arrow, to see if any of the remembered dots would be encountered (right). (from Finke and Pinker 1982)

similar to that obtained in previous image-scanning experiments, where subjects were actually told to scan their images.

These findings were replicated and extended in another set of experiments, in which we manipulated whether or not the subjects were given advance information about where the arrow would appear (Finke and Pinker 1983). We predicted that when given this advance information and sufficient time to make use of it, subjects would not have to rely on image scanning, and their decision times would be independent of the arrow-dot distance. On those trials where advance information about the arrow's location was provided, it was given in the form of a positional cue that was shown two seconds before the onset of the arrow. Figure 3.6 compares the results for conditions in which this positional information was and was not provided. When subjects were uncertain about the arrow's location, their reaction times increased with increasing distance, and the majority of them reported that they had performed the task by imagining that they were scanning along the direction specified by the arrow, to mentally "see" whether any of the dots would be encountered. When they *were* given advance information about the arrow's location, their reaction times were not significantly related to the arrow-

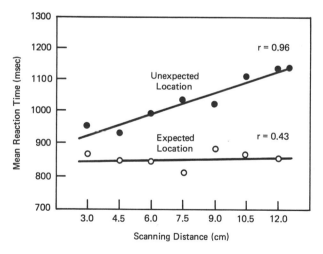

Figure 3.6
Mean reaction time to verify that the arrow was pointing at one of the dots in the previously seen pattern as the distance between the arrow and the dot increased, and depending on whether or not the arrow's location was known in advance. The difference between these reaction time functions suggests that mental image scanning is used whenever one has to judge, from memory, relative directions from unexpected locations. (from Finke and Pinker 1983)

dot distance, and the majority of them reported that they had simply anticipated the correct directions to each of the dots.

Unlike the results of most of the previous experiments on image scanning, these findings are particularly difficult to account for in terms of task demands or tacit knowledge. First, the experimental instructions did not specify that image scanning was to be used, so the subjects were not under any obligation to mentally simulate an actual scan. Second, even if they were intent on simulating an actual scan, there would not have been sufficient time for them to compute the relevant scanning distances in cases where the arrow's location was unexpected. Hence, they could not have used tacit knowledge to govern their response times. In contrast, when they knew in advance where the arrow would be presented, and thus had the opportunity to compute the scanning distances, there was no evidence for image scanning. Evidently, image scanning is the strategy of choice when one has to judge directions among items whose relative positions have not been explicitly encoded.

3.3.2 Spontaneous Image Scanning in Mentally Reconstructed Patterns

Pylyshyn (1984) has argued that by actually presenting the dot patterns and the arrows in these experiments, one artificially "imposes" the spatial properties that are attributed to mental images. This criticism was addressed in a follow-up study by Pinker, Choate, and Finke (1984), which again considered the possibility that task demands might be operating in some subtle way. We repeated the arrow-dot experiment of the Finke and Pinker (1983) study, in which no advance information was given about the arrow's location. This time, however, we allowed the arrow-dot distance to diminish all the way to zero. At the zero scanning distance, there was a dramatic increase in reaction time, whereas the rest of the reaction-time function increased linearly with distance in the usual way. This departure from linearity resulted from small errors in memory for the exact locations of the dots, which made the arrow judgment task extremely difficult when the arrows had been presented at positions adjacent to where the dots had been shown. This effect was not predicted by control subjects, who were given a description of the task and were asked to guess how the response times would vary with distance. Hence it was very unlikely that these results were due to the implicit demands of the experiment.

We then conducted another version of the arrow judgment task in which the subjects judged the arrows while always keeping their eyes closed. They began by learning the locations of three dots in a 10 × 10 square grid. A tape recording then specified the location of the arrow, using Cartesian coordinates, and the direction of the arrow, using a clockwise angle. As before, the subjects were to say whether or not the arrow was pointing to any of the dots in the remembered pattern, and no mention was made of imagery or image scanning. Reaction time increased with increasing scanning distance, except at the minimum distance, where there was again a dramatic departure from linearity. Because no actual displays were used in this experiment, and because the subjects kept their eyes closed during the procedures, these results could not have been explained in terms of externally imposed spatial constraints.

3.3.3 *Imagined Scanning Along Bent and Curved Paths*
Another study that has addressed the possible role of task demands in image-scanning experiments was conducted by Reed, Hock, and Lockhead (1983). They explored mental image scanning along paths that varied in length and shape, while assessing subjects' expectations for how these factors would influence their scanning times. After briefly inspecting the scan path, which consisted of diagonal lines, curved spirals, or bent spirals of varying length (see figure 3.7), the subjects were instructed to close their eyes and to imagine scanning along the path continuously from one end to the other. Their scanning times increased in proportion to the length of the path, but the rate of scanning was slowed as the shape of the path became more complex (see figure 3.8). This was also true when the subjects actually scanned the patterns. When asked to predict the scanning times, control subjects correctly guessed that times would increase with increasing distance (as had been reported by Mitchell and Richman 1980; see section 3.2.3), but they could not guess the

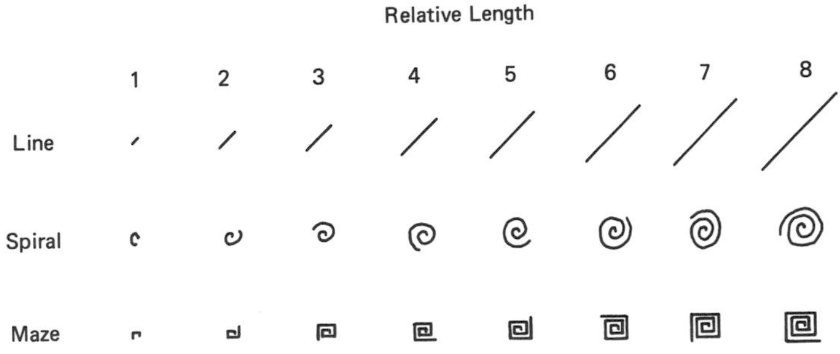

Figure 3.7
Patterns that subjects were to imagine scanning in experiments on varying the length and complexity of the scan path. The numbers at the top indicate the relative length of the patterns. (from Reed, Hock, and Lockhead 1983)

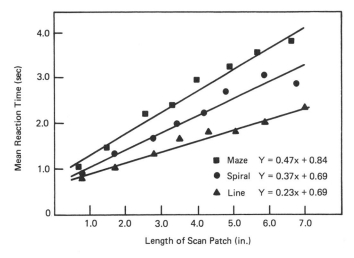

Figure 3.8
Mean reaction time to imagine scanning along the paths shown in figure 3.7, as the length of the paths increased. The different slopes of the functions suggest that the rate of mental image scanning is slowed as the scan path becomes more complex. (from Reed, Hock, and Lockhead 1983)

more subtle effects of the shape of the path on the scanning times. This further argues against accounts based on the task demands of the experiment.

To date, then, image-scanning experiments have provided reasonably good support for the principle of spatial equivalence. Tacit knowledge, task demands, and experimenter bias cannot account for the full range of findings that have been obtained in these experiments. These findings are, therefore, generally consistent with the proposal that mental images preserve the spatial structure of physical paths, surfaces, and spaces.

3.3.4 Mental Image Scanning in the Blind

Nancy Kerr (1983) has demonstrated that mental image scanning is not necessarily based on *visual* imagery. She conducted a tactile version of the Kosslyn, Ball, and Reiser (1978) map-scanning experiment, using congenitally blind subjects. The subjects learned the locations of small objects that were placed on a flat surface; they were able to do this by feeling the objects, as each had a distinctive shape. As in the study by Kosslyn et al., the distances between the objects were varied and there were no intervening objects along any of the scan paths. When a pair of objects were named, the subjects were told to mentally focus on the first object and then to imagine moving a "raised dot" along the surface directly to the second object. Their reaction times, like those in previous image-scanning experiments, were highly correlated with the scanning distances. Mental image scanning can therefore be achieved using purely spatial imagery, having no visual characteristics. (See also section 1.5.4 for related evidence on the use of imagery mnemonics in the blind.)

3.4 Cognitive Maps

The idea that images can serve as mental "maps," depicting the layout of objects in one's environment, is hardly new. The classic experiments of Edward Tolman (1948), for example, showed that after learning to obtain food by following a particular route in a maze, animals could take advantage of short cuts when given the opportunity to do so. This implies that the animals must have formed a spatial representation or *cognitive map* of the maze environment, instead of merely learning a particular sequence of right and left turns. In this section, recent studies exploring the nature of cognitive maps in humans will be considered, as well as the implications of these studies for the principle of spatial equivalence.

3.4.1 Using Mental Images in Spatial Navigation

When planning to go from one place to another, people often imagine the most efficient route. If images do preserve the spatial characteristics of one's environment, it should be possible to use images to discover short cuts that depart from originally learned paths. This should be true even in the absence of visual cues, as long as a person is properly oriented within the environment.

This issue has been explored by Marvin Levine and his colleagues. Levine, Jankovic, and Palij (1982) taught subjects to walk along routes connecting five numbered locations in a large room, while blindfolded. The experimenter guided them along the routes, which required a different turn at each new location (see figure 3.9). The subjects were then placed at one of the locations, while still blindfolded, were oriented toward either the previous or next location along the route, and were asked to walk directly toward *another* location that was designated by its number. For example, the subject might be placed on location 5, facing location 4, and asked to walk directly to location 2. The important finding, shown in figure 3.10, was that the subjects could walk to the designated locations just as accurately when they had to take the direct, novel short cuts as when they could simply walk along the original route. This suggested that they had formed and used a cognitive map of the layout to guide

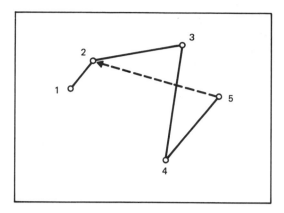

Figure 3.9
Example of routes connecting five numbered locations that subjects learned while blindfolded and being guided by the experimenter. While still blindfolded they were placed on one of the locations, oriented toward the next or previous location along the route, and asked to walk directly toward another location. The dashed line illustrates, for example, the direct route from location 5 to location 2. (from Levine, Jankovic, and Palij 1982)

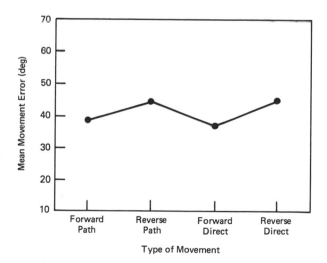

Figure 3.10
Mean angular error in walking from one remembered location to another, depending on whether or not the walk was along the route that was previously used and whether the walk was in the forward or reverse direction with respect to the numbered locations. The equivalence in accuracy for novel, direct movements and movements along the original route suggests that the subjects were using cognitive maps to guide their movements. (from Levine, Jankovic, and Palij 1982)

their movements, in which the relative distances and directions among all the locations were represented, instead of simply having memorized a set of distances and directions that pertained only to the particular route they had previously followed.

The notion that people can rely on mental "maps" when navigating in an experimental environment was further supported by the results of an additional experiment in the same study. The subjects learned the routes by studying actual maps of them and were again blind-folded during the testing phase. This time, their ability to use short cuts to get from one location to another was dramatically affected by whether the map they had studied had been properly aligned with the actual layout: when the map had been read upside down, the subjects made more than seven times as many errors in taking the short cuts as when it had been read right side up. Again, these findings would be hard to explain if all people did was remember distances and turning directions along a route, but they are consistent with the idea that people form cognitive maps that are similar to actual maps.

Another kind of experiment that has explored the use of mental imagery in spatial navigation was conducted by Thomson (1983). In his experiments, subjects walked toward a target on level ground while keeping their eyes closed. As long as the target was not too far away (within about 30 feet) and could be reached in a reasonably short time (within 8 seconds), the subjects were just as accurate in reaching the target as when they did the task while keeping their eyes open. A clever control experiment showed that the subjects were not merely counting their steps as a strategy for keeping track of where they were during the blind walking. They were given a beanbag to carry along and at unexpected points along the path were instructed to stop walking and to throw the bag at the target. Again, they were just as accurate whether they kept their eyes open or closed. Apparently, within certain limits people can navigate simply by imagining where they are located in relation to other objects.

3.4.2 Distortions in Cognitive Maps
The success of any of these experiments obviously depends on a person's ability to form an *accurate* mental image of the locations of objects or places. Spatial relations have to be depicted accurately in an image in order that the image be useful in navigation or in judging relative directions. Studies to be considered next will show, however, that this is not always the case. Rather, there are limitations on the accuracy with which images can preserve spatial relations.

One of the first demonstrations that cognitive maps can be distorted was reported by Lynch (1960). He interviewed residents of several major cities in the United States, such as Boston and Los Angeles, and asked them to describe where various familiar land-marks were located. Often their descriptions were quite inaccurate. For example, prominent buildings in the cities were typically misre-membered as being arranged in simple north-south or east-west configurations. This had the consequence that residents of the cities would often become disoriented when they departed from familiar routes. Sadalla, Burroughs, and Staplin (1980) have also demon-strated that errors in the way familiar landmarks are remembered can lead to distortions in cognitive maps.

Stevens and Coupe (1978) have shown that cognitive maps for the relative locations of cities can be distorted by familiar relations among large-scale or "superordinant" regions that surround the cities. Con-sider, for example, the following question: Which is farther west, Reno, Nevada, or San Diego, California? Most people would say that San Diego is farther west, when in fact Reno is the correct answer. The reason such errors are made, according to Stevens and Coupe, is that cognitive maps are distorted by our knowledge about how the surrounding regions are related; knowing that California is supposed to be west of Nevada, for example. Similarly, Barbara Tyersky (1981) has shown that memories for the relative locations of landmarks that are in different geographic regions are often shifted according to beliefs people have about how those regions are aligned. For exam-ple, contrary to what most people believe, North America is not directly north of South America, but is actually northwest of it. Hence, it seems surprising to discover that Florida is actually west of Chile.

These demonstrations call into question whether the principle of spatial equivalence is always valid. Apparently, images of the loca-tions of objects and places can sometimes be distorted. This situation is similar to that discussed in chapter 1, where the notion that images were "pictorial" had to be qualified. Recall that various studies had showed that mental images of how objects looked could be distorted by the way the objects were initially interpreted (see section 1.5.3). However, these studies also showed that images could still have demonstrable, pictorial-like properties, despite these distortions. The same appears to be true of cognitive maps.

For example, Kosslyn, Pick, and Fariello (1974) had subjects learn the locations of objects that were separated into four regions by transparent or opaque barriers. Cognitive maps that were based on the learned locations were accurate within each region and between regions separated by transparent barriers, but were distorted between regions separated by opaque barriers, in which case distances crossing the barriers were overestimated. Despite these distortions, however, the cognitive maps still preserved the essential spatial relations that were contained in the original configuration of objects.

In a related study, Perry Thorndyke (1981) found that cognitive maps consisting of a system of routes can be distorted by increasing the number of intervening locations along the routes. This suggested that filled distances on cognitive maps are "expanded" relative to empty distances. Figure 3.11 shows one of the maps that subjects learned in these experiments. Their task was to estimate, from memory, distances along the routes connecting two designated locations. As shown in figure 3.12, the distance estimates increased in proportion to the lengths of the routes and, independently, in proportion to the number of locations encountered along the routes. In agreement with the findings of Kosslyn, Ball, and Reiser (1978), Thorndyke also found that rates of mental image scanning along these same routes increased, independently, with both distance and the number of intervening locations (see section 3.1.1). These findings also suggest that even though distances represented in cognitive maps can

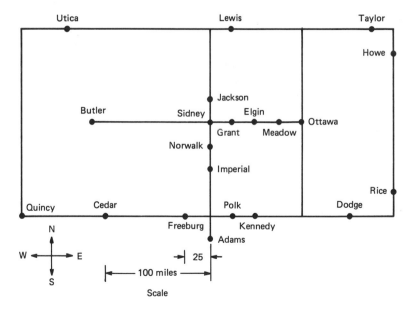

Figure 3.11
Example of fictional maps used in experiments on estimating, from memory, distances between cities along specific routes connecting the cities. (from Thorndyke 1981)

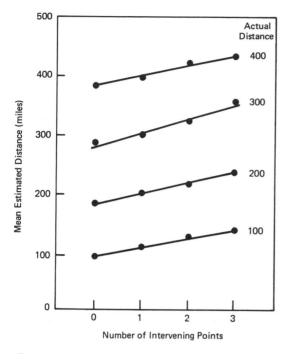

Figure 3.12
Mean estimated distance between cities connected by particular routes, recalled from memory, as the number of other cities along the routes increased and as the actual distance between the cities increased. The independence of these two effects shows that even when cognitive maps are distorted, remembered distances are still proportional to the corresponding distances on actual maps. (from Thorndyke 1981)

be distorted, the cognitive maps still preserve much of the spatial structure of actual maps.

A comprehensive study of the structure of cognitive maps was carried out recently by Timothy McNamara (1986). His subjects began by learning random configurations of objects that were divided into four distinct regions. Their memory for the layouts was then tested using one of three methods. First, the subjects were given the names of the objects in a recognition test, after having been "primed" with the name of some other object in the same layout. Presumably, increased priming of the recalled object would reflect shorter distances between the objects in the memory representations. Second, the subjects were given one of the objects and were asked to make directional judgments to a second, named object. Third, they were given pairs of objects and were asked to estimate the distance between the objects. All three measures converged to suggest the following: although distances in cognitive maps can be systematically distorted by the presence of boundaries, the cognitive maps still exhibit many of the spatial characteristics of actual maps.

Taken together, these findings indicate that cognitive maps would provide accurate representations of geographic regions only when the regions were relatively free of boundaries or other salient landmarks. The principle of spatial equivalence must be similarly qualified. Even when cognitive maps are distorted in this way, however, they still correspond to actual maps in which the locations have been slightly rearranged.

3.4.3 Inconsistencies in Judgments of Relative Direction

There is one further problem with the notion that a cognitive map faithfully represents an actual layout or map. When subjects judge relative directions between locations on a remembered layout, their judgments sometimes suggest *impossible* configurations. Moar and Bower (1983), for example, asked subjects to judge the relative directions between pairs of familiar towns and found that their judgments were often nonsymmetrical. For instance, if one town were judged as being northeast of a second, the second town might not be judged as being southwest of the first. Likewise, Baird, Wagner, and Noma (1982) have found that subjects' estimates of distances between locations in a cognitive map sometimes suggest geometrical configurations that could never actually exist. Such findings suggest that cognitive maps may not always be internally consistent.

3.5 Spatial Representations in Long-Term Memory

One might wonder whether cognitive maps are ever actually *stored* in memory, in a kind of spatial "format," or are they merely constructed for temporary use from more abstract forms of knowledge about objects and their locations? For that matter, do spatial representations of *any* sort exist in long-term memory?

3.5.1 Spatial Structures Revealed by Multidimensional Scaling

These are difficult questions, because the representational structures in long-term memory, unlike mental images, do not lend themselves to being "inspected" or "scanned" (see sections 1.5.5; 2.2.5). A promising approach, however, has made use of a technique called *multidimensional scaling*. This technique can reveal information about the structure of memory representations that underlie what are called *judgments of proximity* (see Shepard 1980). Typically, one is asked to rate the similarity of all possible pairs of items in a large stimulus set. These similarity judgments are then analyzed using computer programs that assess whether the ratings can be accounted for by placing the items at locations within a multidimensional "space." If so, one has evidence that the underlying memory representation possesses a similar type of spatial structure.

Consider, for example, how multidimensional scaling could allow you to determine the spatial structure of a map of the United States, if all you knew were the distances between pairs of the major U.S. cities. The scaling program would attempt to "fit" these distances to spatial representations of increasing dimensionality. For instance, a one-dimensional solution would not work, since the major U.S. cities do not all lie along a single straight line. In contrast, a two-dimensional solution, in which the cities would be represented as points on a flat surface, would account very well for these distances. A three-dimensional solution, which would take into account the curvature of the earth, would be only marginally better. In this way, multidimensional scaling would reveal the spatial configuration from which distances between the cities were derived.

This same technique has been used to explore the spatial structure of cognitive maps, based on a person's estimates of distances among pairs of objects or places. These estimated distances can then be accounted for in terms of two- or three-dimensional scaling solutions corresponding approximately to actual physical layouts or to slightly distorted versions of them (Baird 1979; Evans 1980; Kosslyn, Pick, and Fariello 1974). Such findings, however, do not necessarily show that the long-term memory representations that are used in generating spatial images exhibit these same spatial characteristics. For all one knows, these underlying memory representations might consist simply of a "list" of known distances, which are then used in constructing the spatial images or cognitive maps.

A more convincing demonstration of the existence of spatial representations in long-term memory would be to show that other kinds of similarity judgments not involving *physical* distance per se can also be accounted for in terms of the spatial solutions of multidimensional scaling. An example comes from an experiment by Shepard and Chipman (1970). They had subjects rank the similarity of the shapes of pairs of selected U.S. states. This was done in one of two ways. In one condition, the subjects were shown outlined drawings of the states in making each comparison. In another condition, they were merely given the names of the states and had to make the comparisons from memory. After the subjects ranked each pair in order from most to least similar in shape, the rankings were subjected to multidimensional scaling. The use of judgments of similarity in shape, as opposed to physical distance, has the advantage that the subjects were unlikely to have had prior knowledge about the particular "distances" involved. For each condition, the similarity judgments could be accounted for by corresponding two-dimensional solutions, suggesting that information about relative shape is stored in long-term memory in the form of spatial representations.

3.5.2 Correspondences Between Physical and Representational Dimensions

Related findings suggesting that spatial representations exist in long-term memory have been reported for similarity judgments involving faces (Gordon and Hayward 1973), numerical symbols (Shepard, Kilpatric, and Cunningham 1975), and colors (see Shepard 1975). In general, the dimensions in these scaling solutions correspond to the salient physical dimensions of the objects or patterns. This correspondence between the spatial structure of memories for objects and shapes, as revealed by multidimensional scaling, and the spatial structure of their actual geometric or physical characteristics led Shepard to propose a principle for long-term memory representations, which he called the *principle of the second-order isomorphism*. This principle states that relations among internal representations correspond to relations among the associated external objects (Shepard and Chipman 1970). This is to be contrasted with a "first-order" isomorphism between internal representations and external objects. For example, the underlying memory representation for the shape of a square need not actually be "squarelike," but it should be more similar to memory representations for geometric forms that are similar to squares than to memory representations for shapes that are very different from squares. These relationships among the memory representations are, presumably, the "spatial" structures that are revealed by multidimensional scaling.

3.6 Summary and Conclusions

The principle of spatial equivalence has received strong support from studies on the imagined scanning of objects and on the use of cognitive maps in spatial navigation. As a rule, spatial relations among objects are preserved in images, although sometimes these relations can be distorted. The spatial structure of images also extends to the third dimension, as shown by studies on imagined scanning in depth. Although image scanning has been used primarily as a technique for measuring distances that are represented in images, it also has the practical function of enabling one to judge spatial relations that have not been previously learned. Whether or not spatial representations also exist in long-term memory is debatable, although studies on multidimensional scaling have provided some supporting evidence.

3.7 Further Explorations

3.7.1 Recommendations for Further Reading
Additional information on image-scanning experiments can be found in Kosslyn's *Image and Mind* (1980), and in articles by Kosslyn (1981) and Pylyshyn (1981). Halpern (in press) has recently extended the image-scanning paradigm to investigate the imagined auditory scanning of musical notes. For further references on cognitive maps, see reviews by Downs and Stea (1977), Evans (1980), Lynch (1960), and Olton (1977). Reviews of additional applications of multidimensional scaling, including its use in uncovering memory representations for music and semantic relations, can be found in articles by Hutchinson and Lockhead (1977), Krumhansl and Kessler (1982), and Shepard (1980, 1982). Alternatives to using multidimensional scaling have been discussed in articles by Shepard and Arabie (1979) and Tversky (1977).

3.7.2 Visual "Routines" That Resemble Image Scanning
Shimon Ullman (1984) has proposed that the visual system employs various high-speed scanning operations, called visual *routines*, to rapidly integrate spatial information across the visual field. One of these routines, "curve tracing," appears to resemble mental image scanning. Jolicoeur, Ullman, and Mackay (1986) presented subjects with displays consisting of a set of nonoverlapping curved lines and asked them to verify that two X marks were on the same line. The time it took them to do so increased as the marks were further displaced along the lines. Because the displays were presented for durations that were too short to permit the subjects actually to scan the lines with their eyes, this suggests that they had "internally" scanned them. It remains to be seen, however, whether scanning carried out in visual routines is the same process people use when they imagine that they are scanning along a remembered path (see section 3.4.2).

3.7.3 Using Mental "Rulers" to Measure Distance
There is evidence that people can estimate distances by imagining that they are laying out a mental "ruler" of constant length. Hartley (1977) asked subjects to estimate the lengths of a set of lines by giving

their estimates in terms of a standard "unit" length. The time it took them to make these estimates increased in proportion to the lengths of the lines. When the length of the standard was then increased, it took them proportionally less time to make these same judgments (Hartley 1981). Unknown distances might therefore be estimated by measuring out the distances in imagination.

Chapter 4

Transformations of Mental Images

Up to now, we have considered characteristics of mental images that are essentially "static"—for example, the way an image "looks" or the way parts are "arranged" in an image. However, imagery can also be a dynamic process. One can visualize objects moving, events unfolding, and forms changing shape. These "transformational" properties of images, and the scientific methods that have been developed to study them, will be the topic of the present chapter.

4.1 Mental Rotation

One of the fascinating things people can do in imagery is to imagine turning objects around. This can be very useful. For example, what would the lower-case letter p look like if it were turned upside down? Most people claim that they imagine rotating the letter to find out. This first section will describe experiments that have explored the imagined rotation of objects, which is commonly referred to as "mental rotation."

4.1.1 Imagined Rotations of Three-Dimensional Objects
The classic study on mental rotation was conducted by Roger Shepard and Jacqueline Metzler (1971). They presented subjects with pairs of perspective line drawings of three-dimensional forms constructed out of small cubes, such as those shown in figure 4.1. The forms were either identical in shape or were mirror-image reversals of one another and could differ by rotations either in the picture plane or in depth. The subjects' task was to verify whether or not the forms were identical in shape, despite any differences in orientation. Shepard and Metzler predicted that when the forms differed in orientation, the subjects would have to imagine rotating one of the forms into alignment with the other to compare their shapes and that this should take longer as the angular distance between the forms increased. Because the shapes of the forms differed by mirror-

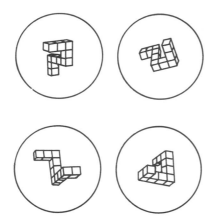

Figure 4.1
Example of pairs of perspective line drawings of three-dimensional forms that were either identical in shape or mirror-image reversals. The subjects were to judge the equivalence of the shapes of the forms, irrespective of the depicted differences in their orientation. (from Shepard and Metzler 1971)

image reflections, the subjects could not simply rely on single, distinctive features of the forms in making their judgments.

The results of the Shepard and Metzler experiment are shown in figure 4.2. For rotations in both the picture plane and in depth, the time it took to verify that the forms were equivalent increased in direct proportion to the angular differences between the forms. Moreover, the rate of increase was the same for both types of rotations. These findings had two important implications. First, the proportional increase in response time implied that the imagined rotations must have been carried out at a constant rate for all the comparisons. Second, because the rates of imagined rotation were the same for angular disparities in the picture plane and in depth, what was imagined as rotating must have been the three-dimensional objects, not the two-dimensional pictures of them. In these respects, imagined rotations correspond to actual physical rotations of objects.

4.1.2 Imagined Rotations of Alphanumeric Characters
A subsequent study by Lynn Cooper and Shepard (1973b) explored the use of mental rotation in identifying rotated letters and numbers. The structure of their experiment is illustrated in figure 4.3. The subjects were first presented with an outlined drawing of the letter or number to be identified, in its standard, upright orientation. On most of the trials they were then shown an arrow, for a duration ranging from 100 to 1000 milliseconds, that indicated the orientation

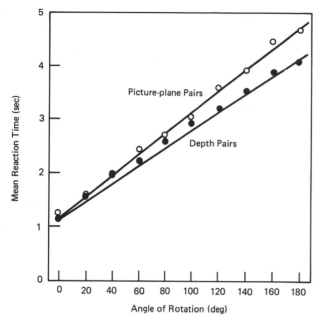

Figure 4.2
Mean reaction time to verify that the three-dimensional forms illustrated in figure 4.1 had the same shape, as the depicted orientations of the forms differed by rotations in the picture plane and in depth. The linear dependence of reaction time on angular disparity suggests that the subjects had imagined rotating the forms into congruence before judging their shapes. The similar slopes of the functions suggest that the imagined rotations were performed using the three-dimensional objects, rather than the two-dimensional pictures. (from Shepard and Metzler 1971)

of a forthcoming test character, which would immediately follow the arrow. Their task was to verify whether the test character was the normal or reflected version of the initially presented character. Their verification times, presented in figure 4.4, were again suggestive of mental rotation. In those cases where the subjects had not been given the orientation cue, or had insufficient time to make use of it, the response times increased as the test character was rotated by increasing amounts from its standard orientation. In contrast, when they had been given a full second to prepare for the test character, their reaction-time functions were essentially flat, suggesting that they had then been able to complete the imagined rotations before the test character appeared.

Cooper and Shepard (1973a) also performed a version of this experiment in which subjects were given the orientation cue in advance, with adequate preparation time, but without knowing the

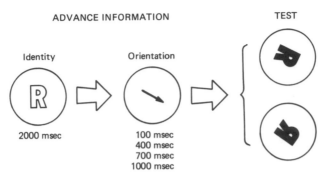

Figure 4.3
Structure of trial sequences used in experiments on identifying rotated alphanumeric characters. After being presented with an outlined drawing of the character in its standard orientation, subjects were shown an arrow indicating the orientation of a forthcoming test character, which they were to judge as being the normal or reflected version of the initially presented character. (from Cooper and Shepard 1973b)

identity of the test character. In this case, their verification times increased with increasing rotation of the test character, just as when no information about orientation had been provided. This suggests that what subjects are doing in these tasks is imagining the rotation of a concrete object or pattern, and not some abstract frame of reference for orientation. A similar finding was later reported by Cooper and Shepard (1975) for identifying rotated drawings of right and left hands; providing orientation cues without identity cues was not helpful. Evidently, these tasks are performed by carrying out a mental analog to the actual rotation of a concrete object.

Two other aspects of the Cooper and Shepard experiments are worth noting. First, the subjects could perform the mental rotations in either the clockwise or counterclockwise direction, depending on which provided the shortest angular distance to the standard, upright orientation. This is why the reaction-time function in figure 4.4 reached a peak at the 180-degree rotation. Also, the reaction times in these studies did not increase in strict proportion to increasing rotation from the upright. The reason, as subsequent studies have shown, is that most alphanumeric characters are regarded as being "upright" even when slightly tilted, making it unnecessary to carry out the mental rotations for small amounts of rotation (Hock and Tromley 1978). In contrast, the reaction-time functions are strikingly linear when the stimulus patterns have no natural upright orientation, as shown by the Shepard and Metzler (1971) study and by additional studies to be considered shortly.

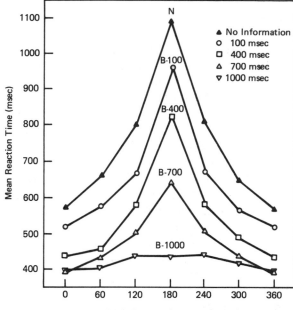

Figure 4.4
Mean reaction time for judging the test character as it was rotated clockwise from the standard orientation, and as subjects were given increasing amounts of preparation time following presentation of the arrow. The progressive flattening of the reaction time functions with additional preparation time suggests that the subjects had performed the task by imagining that the initial character was rotated into congruence with the test character along the shortest rotational path. (from Cooper and Shepard 1973b)

4.2 The Principle of Transformational Equivalence

These findings suggest that mental rotation resembles the actual rotation of concrete objects or patterns. Our fourth principle, the *principle of transformational equivalence,* makes a general proposal about the relation between imagined transformations and their physical counterparts:

Imagined transformations and physical transformations exhibit corresponding dynamic characteristics and are governed by the same laws of motion.

This principle leads to a number of predictions that have been tested using the mental rotation paradigm. These will be considered in the remainder of this section.

4.2.1 *The Holistic Character of Mental Rotation*

One implication of the principle of transformational equivalence is that mental rotations should involve the imagined rotation of whole, completed objects. In other words, the mental rotations should be holistic, as opposed to being carried out in some fragmented, piece-meal fashion—where, for example, one might imagine rotating an object a piece at a time. Further, the mental rotations should not depend on the visual *complexity* of the object or pattern. Physical rotations, by analogy, do not slow up or break down just because an object happens to have many features or parts. The same should be true of mental rotations.

Experimental demonstrations of the holistic character of mental rotation have been reported by Cooper (1975). She used a technique for varying the complexity of patterns that was developed earlier by Attneave and Arnoult (1956). As shown in figure 4.5, the stimuli consisted of polygons that were formed by connecting a randomly distributed set of points, where complexity was varied by varying the number of points. The subjects were first trained to discriminate normal from reflected versions of these random polygons at some particular orientation. They were then shown the polygons at orientations that departed from the trained orientation, where it was

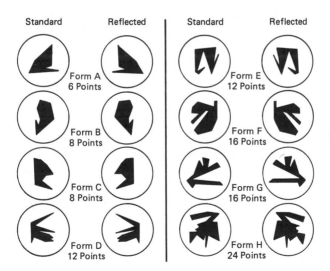

Figure 4.5
Examples of normal and reflected versions of random polygons and the method used to vary their complexity. Subjects learned each polygon at a single, "trained" orientation and were then shown test patterns at various orientations that departed from the trained orientation in 60-degree steps. (from Cooper 1975)

expected that mental rotation would be needed to make the discriminations. Cooper predicted that if mental rotation is indeed a holistic process, the rotation rates should not depend on the complexity of the patterns. The results of this study, presented in figure 4.6, confirmed this prediction: the reaction times increased linearly with increasing departure from the trained orientation, and the rate of increase was independent of the patterns' complexity.

Cooper and Podgorny (1976) provided further evidence that the subjects in this experiment were not merely imagining the rotation of only certain parts of the patterns in making their discriminations. In addition to using reflected versions of the polygons as distractors, they included test patterns that differed in similarity from the targets by varying degrees. The latter distractors consisted of graded perturbations of the target patterns formed by randomly displacing one or more of the vertexes in the patterns. Cooper and Podgorny found that the mental rotation rates were independent not only of the complexity of the patterns, but also of how similar the test forms were to the target forms. This implies that the imagined rotations were of the whole, completed forms, and not merely of specific portions of them. Had the subjects imagined rotating only certain parts of the patterns, the mental rotation rates would have increased with increasing similarity between the target forms and the distractors. (However, see Anderson 1978 for other possible explanations for these findings.)

4.2.2 The Analog Character of Mental Rotation

A second implication of the principle of transformational equivalence is that mental transformations, like physical transformations, should be *continuous*. Mental rotations, for example, should not occur as discrete sequences of static images that are successively rotated in a stepwise fashion but should be carried out in a smooth and continuous manner. That is, as Cooper and Shepard (1973a, 1978) proposed, mental rotations, like actual rotations, should pass through all the intermediate points along the transformational path. So for example, if a person imagines rotating a pattern 90 degrees clockwise from the upright position, the imagined rotation should pass through all the orientations in between 0 and 90 degrees.

This proposed continuity of mental rotation was tested by Cooper (1976a). She began by using subjects whose individual rates of mental rotation were known from her previous experiments. These subjects were shown the random polygons in one of six orientations that they were already familiar with, which ranged from 0 to 360 degrees in 60-degree steps. As soon as the pattern was removed, they were to

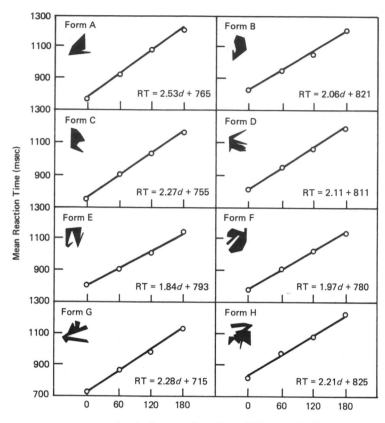

Figure 4.6
Mean reaction time to compare rotated versions of the polygons illustrated in figure
4.5, as the difference between the presented orientations and the trained orientations
increased. The linear dependence of reaction time on angular disparity suggests that
the subjects had imagined rotating the standard and test patterns into congruence,
whereas the equivalence of the slopes of the functions suggests that the rates of
mental rotation were independent of the complexity of the patterns. (from Cooper
1975)

begin imagining that it was rotating clockwise at their normal rate of mental rotation. Some time thereafter a test pattern was presented, either at one of the six familiar orientations (at 0, 60, 120 degrees), or at one of six orientations exactly *in between* those (at 30, 90, 150 degrees). These intermediate orientations were unexpected and were included to determine whether the mental rotations would also "pass" through them. As before, the subjects indicated whether the test pattern was the normal or reflected version of the starting pattern.

The reaction times increased linearly with increasing departure of the test pattern orientation from where the mentally rotated pattern should have been at that time, based on the subject's normal rate of mental rotation. This was true whether the test patterns were presented at the previously trained orientations or at the unfamiliar orientations, which implied that mental rotations are at least approximately continuous, and pass through at least some of the intermediate points along the rotational path.

4.2.3 *Imagined Transformations of Size*
Mental transformations of a different sort can be used to compare objects that are presented at different *sizes*. Bundesen and Larsen (1975) presented subjects with pairs of random polygons, similar to those used by Cooper (1975), that were identical in shape but could differ in orientation or size. The subjects were to say whether or not the two polygons were identical in orientation, irrespective of their size differences. Response time increased in proportion to increasing changes in the size ratios, suggesting that they had performed the task by imagining one of the patterns increasing or decreasing in size at a constant rate to match the size of the other pattern. Larsen and Bundesen (1978) then extended this finding to cases where the patterns were presented sequentially. They found that the linear increase in reaction times with increasing size ratios could not be explained simply in terms of adjusting an abstract, mental "frame" of reference for size. As in the mental rotation experiments of Cooper and Shepard (1973b), evidence for mental transformations was obtained only when the subjects could imagine the specific, concrete pattern.

What would happen if a mental size transformation were combined with a mental rotation? Several studies have suggested that the two types of transformations would be carried out independently. For example, Sekuler and Nash (1972) showed subjects pairs of rectangles that differed in both relative size and orientation; the subjects had to say whether or not the rectangles had the same shape, irrespective of their other differences. Reaction time increased, independently, with increases in size ratio and orientation differences. A similar effect was reported by Bundesen, Larsen, and Farrell (1981) for pairs of alphanumeric characters. These findings suggest that mental size transformations can be performed prior to, after, or in alternation with mental rotations, but not at the same time. The issue of how mental rotations and mental size transformations are combined appears to be somewhat more complicated, however, because mental size transformations may not have to be performed at all when the stimuli are sufficiently different in shape (see Besner and Coltheart 1976; Kubovy and Podgorny 1981).

4.2.4 Imagined Transformations of Shape and Color

People are also capable of carrying out mental transformations that correspond to more complex types of physical transformations. For example, Shepard and Feng (1972) demonstrated that two-dimensional patterns could be mentally "folded" to make three-dimensional forms. They presented subjects with patterns made up of connected squares, such as those shown in figure 4.7. The subjects' task was to determine, using the shaded square as the stationary base, whether the edges of the two squares that were designated by the arrows would touch if the squares were folded to make a cube. Their reaction times increased in proportion to the total number of squares that would have been carried along in a sequence of actual folds; this suggested that they had performed the task by imagining that the patterns were actually being folded. This was also true when pairs of the patterns were shown already partially folded and the subjects had to say whether the patterns could be further folded into precise congruence (Bassman 1978).

In general, it may be necessary to imagine transforming a pattern

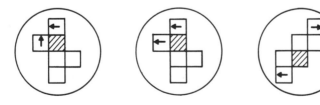

Figure 4.7
Examples of stimuli used in experiments on the imagined folding of patterns into three-dimensional shapes. The subjects were supposed to verify, using the shaded square as a stationary base, whether the edges of the squares designated by the arrows would touch if the squares were folded into a cube. The time it took them to do so increased with increasing number of squares that would have been carried along in actual folds of the patterns. (from Shepard and Feng 1972)

to compensate mentally for differences along dimensions that are irrelevant to the judgment task. As an example, Dixon and Just (1978) presented subjects with pairs of ellipses that differed in width and height and asked them to compare the ellipses along one dimension (width) while ignoring the other dimension (height). The subjects' reaction times increased with increasing differences along the irrelevant dimension. Dixon and Just obtained a similar finding for patterns differing in color, where the subjects were to judge differences either in hue or in tint. Again, reaction time increased when the patterns differed by increasing amounts along the irrelevant dimension. The findings suggest, therefore, that one of the purposes of performing a mental transformation is to *normalize* stimuli along irrelevant dimensions prior to comparing them along relevant dimensions.

To summarize, these various findings provide convergent support for the principle of transformational equivalence. Like actual physical transformations, mental transformations are evidently performed in a holistic and continuous manner. In addition, mental transformations may correspond to many different types of physical transformations, including changes in color or shape. Note, incidentally, that the typical increase in reaction time with increasing stimulus differences in these tasks is the *opposite* of the symbolic distance effect, which was discussed in section 1.3.3. Recall that this effect refers to an increase in reaction time with *decreasing* differences between the stimuli. The symbolic distance effect, however, has to do with differences along the *relevant* dimensions of comparison, whereas the effects of mental transformations under discussion here pertain to differences along *irrelevant* dimensions.

4.3 Criticisms of the Mental Rotation Experiments

These conclusions about the dynamic characteristics of mental imagery have not been universally accepted. This section will examine criticisms of these studies and will consider additional findings that suggest other possible interpretations.

4.3.1 Exceptions to the Holistic-Analog Hypothesis

If mental rotations really are carried out continuously, and in a holistic manner, then the mental rotation rates ought not to depend on any of the visual characteristics of the mentally rotated patterns. The findings of Hochberg and Gellman (1977) suggest that this might not always be true. They presented subjects with pairs of patterns that varied in how easily landmark features for the patterns' identity and

orientation could be distinguished. These landmark features consisted of small lines that extended orthogonally from the major axes
of the patterns. Hochberg and Gellman found that the rates of mental
rotation were reduced as the landmark features became more salient.
In a related study, Pylyshyn (1979) presented subjects with line drawings, together with rotated test patterns, and asked them to say
whether or not the test patterns were a part of the line drawings.
The estimated mental rotation rates depended on whether the test
patterns constituted "good" parts of the line drawings, as assessed
by subjects' ratings of the parts. These results suggested that mental
rotation may sometimes be carried out in a piecemeal manner, giving
precedence to an object's salient, distinctive features.

Shepard and Cooper (1982) have pointed out, however, that neither of these studies properly controlled for possible differences in
how easily the stimuli could have been encoded or compared at the
presented orientations. For example, in Pylyshyn's study, the rated
"goodness" of the parts was confounded with the orientation at
which the parts were presented. In addition, because the stimuli
used in these studies were unfamiliar to the subjects, they might
have been unable to form complete mental images of them. This is
in contrast to the extensive training procedures employed by Cooper
(1975) and by Cooper and Podgorny (1976), who found that the
mental rotation rates were independent of the visual complexity of
the patterns (see again section 4.2.1). There is also evidence that
when subjects are specifically told to attend to only one part of a
complex pattern, their mental rotation rates differ from those where
they are specifically told to attend to the entire pattern (Robertson
and Palmer 1983; Yuille and Steiger 1982). Finally, Bethell-Fox and
Shepard (1988) have shown that pattern complexity affects mental
rotation rates when subjects begin to use a novel set of patterns, but
not after they become familiar with the patterns. Thus, only when
subjects are unable to form a complete mental image of the stimulus
patterns, or when they are motivated not to do so, are mental rotations performed in a piecemeal fashion.

A further objection to the Hochberg and Gellman study is that
when salient features or landmarks are included in the presented
stimuli, one might be able to distinguish their shapes without having
to perform mental rotations at all. To take an extreme example, one
could easily distinguish the letter X from the letter O without ever
having to imagine the characters rotated into congruence. In fact,
this was the point of using mirror-image distractors in earlier studies
on mental rotation, so that subjects could not simply rely on the

individual parts of the patterns when comparing them (see again section 4.1.1).

Of course, there may be situations where a person can mentally "skip ahead" when imagining an event, as when one imagines an extended activity such as driving to the grocery store or walking around the block (see Pylyshyn 1981). It should therefore be possible, at least in principle, to form a mental image of an object at unfamiliar orientations without first having to imagine it being rotated from some standard orientation, by imagining how the object's parts would have to be positioned. This may require too much time, however, to be a useful strategy in most experiments on mental rotation, which require rapid discriminations. (See also the related discussion, in section 3.2.1, of the relative efficiency of "blink" vs. "scan" strategies for locating features in images.)

4.3.2 Evidence for the Mental Rotation of Abstract Reference Frames
A further criticism of mental rotation studies concerns the claim that mental rotations, and other kinds of mental transformations, must always be performed on a concrete image of some specific object. Robertson, Palmer, and Gomez (1987) have recently demonstrated that, under certain conditions, subjects can apparently use an abstract frame of reference to distinguish normal from reflected letters. In one of their experiments, the subjects were first shown a square array consisting of four letters. The letters were identical and had the same form (normal or reflected), and the entire array was rotated by 90 degrees. Shortly thereafter, a single, target letter was presented in normal or reflected form, which could differ from the letters in the array. When the orientation of the target letter matched that of the rotated array, there was a small but significant reduction in the time it took to identify the form of the target letter, suggesting that the array had provided a helpful reference frame. However, this "frame" effect was quite small, and other studies have shown that it is virtually eliminated if the time between presentations of the frame and the target exceeds 100 milliseconds (Koriat and Norman 1984, 1988).

4.3.3 Contribution of Eye Movements
The possible role that eye movements might play in mental rotation experiments also needs to be assessed. For instance, Just and Carpenter (1976, 1985) have found that subjects make an increasing number of eye movements between the corresponding parts of rotated patterns as the angular difference between the patterns increases. Such findings suggest that the linear increase in reaction time with increasing angular difference, usually regarded as evidence

for mental rotation, may simply be an artifact of the number of eye movements performed in comparing the stimuli. This eye movement account, however, could not explain the results of mental rotation experiments in which the stimuli are presented *successively* (Cooper 1975; Cooper and Podgorny 1976), which yield reaction-time functions that also increase in a linear fashion with increasing angular disparity. (See section 2.4.4 for a discussion of how eye movements can create artifacts in other kinds of imagery experiments.)

4.3.4 Inconsistency in the Rate of Mental Rotation
A comparison of the reaction-time functions in figures 4.2 and 4.6 shows that the rates of mental rotation in the R. Shepard and J. Metzler (1971) study were on the order of 60 degrees per second, whereas those in the Cooper (1975) study were much faster, on the order of 500 degrees per second. As critics of these experiments have argued (Pylyshyn 1978, 1981), this inconsistency calls for an explanation. S. Shepard and D. Metzler (1988) have recently shown that this difference in the rate of mental rotation is due to differences in the way the stimuli were presented in these two studies (simultaneously vs. successively). Presumably, with successive presentation, subjects can form a completed memory image of the first stimulus before the second stimulus appears, which makes it easier to carry out the mental rotation.

4.3.5 Task Demands and Tacit Knowledge
It would seem that experiments on mental rotation are less susceptible to criticisms based on task demands and tacit knowledge, because in most cases the subjects are never told to imagine simulating physical motions. Even so, they could still be influenced by more subtle aspects of these tasks, such as the way the stimuli are presented or the expectations of the experimenter (Intons-Peterson 1983; Pylyshyn 1981). Later in this chapter, I will consider studies that argue against these and other such accounts of the findings on mental rotation.

4.4 Extensions of the Mental Rotation Paradigm

Mental rotation experiments have been extended in other practical and theoretically significant ways.

4.4.1 Judging Relative Directions from Imagined Changes in Orientation
People often claim that they can imagine how objects would look from different points of view (Huttenlocher and Presson 1973; see

also the experiments by Pinker 1980 on changing perspective in mental image scanning, discussed in section 3.1.2). Some recent studies have explored the extent to which mental rotation might be used in conjunction with these imagined changes in perspective. Hintzman, O'Dell, and Arndt (1981) presented subjects with a target dot that could appear in one of eight positions around a circle, together with an arrow that was pointing radially to one of these positions (see figure 4.8). The subjects were to imagine that they were placed at the center of the circle, facing the direction specified by the arrow, and to indicate where the target dot would be in relation to themselves. Their reaction times for giving the target directions increased as the arrow was further rotated from the upright position, suggesting that they had performed the task by first imagining that the entire display was rotated to that position.

A related finding by Shepard and Hurwitz (1984) showed that people can use mental rotation to distinguish right from left turns in a rotated display. The subjects were first shown a "standard" line at some orientation, onto which a shorter line segment was then added, representing a right or left turn. The time it took the subjects to identify the type of turn increased with increasing departure of the standard line from the upright position. In this study, as well as in that by Hintzman et al., the subjects derived little benefit from having been given the orientation information in advance, unless they were also given more specific information about the nature of the stimulus.

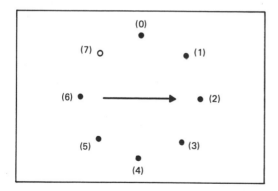

Figure 4.8
Stimulus configuration used in experiments on imagining changes in bodily orientation. The subjects were to imagine facing the direction indicated by the arrow and then to determine where a target dot, presented at one of eight positions, would be in relation to their imagined viewing perspective. Their response times increased as the arrow was further rotated from the upright position, suggesting that they had used mental rotation to perform the task. (from Hintzman, O'Dell, and Arndt 1981)

This further argues against the value of imagining the rotation of an abstract frame of reference (see section 4.3.2). As one practical implication, these findings suggest that mental rotation may be helpful in judging directions on maps that are turned around, where the maps cannot be physically rotated. (See also the related study by Levine, Jankovic, and Palij 1982, on spatial navigation using mental maps, which was discussed in section 3.4.1.)

4.4.2 Detecting Symmetry in Rotated Patterns

Corballis and Roldan (1975) found that mental rotation can be used to judge whether or not a pattern possesses mirror symmetry. Their subjects were shown dot patterns, at various orientations, that either were or were not bilaterally symmetrical. The time it took them to verify that the patterns were symmetrical increased as the axis of symmetry was increasingly rotated from the vertical. This suggested that they had made their judgments by first imagining that the patterns were rotated back to that standard orientation. They were not helped by knowing in advance only what the orientation of the patterns would be, without also knowing what the patterns would look like.

4.4.3 Mental Rotation in the Blind

Mental rotation, like mental image scanning (see section 3.3.4), need not always be based on *visual* imagery. Marmor and Zaback (1976) found that when congenitally blind subjects compared normal and mirror-reversed patterns that were presented at different orientations on a raised surface, their discrimination times increased with increasing angular disparity, although at a slower rate than for sighted subjects. Carpenter and Eisenberg (1978) reported a similar finding using haptically presented letters. Mental rotations can thus be performed using purely spatial imagery. The principle of transformational equivalence, like the principle of spatial equivalence, is therefore not restricted to any one sensory modality.

4.4.4 Biomechanical Constraints in Mental Rotation

A recent series of experiments by Lawrence Parsons (1987a, 1987b) have revealed that mental rotations involving parts of the body are influenced by biomechanical constraints that would be imposed on the corresponding bodily movements. In one experiment (Parsons 1987b), subjects were shown drawings of either the front or the back of a right or left hand. The subjects reported that in order to identify the type of hand it was, they had to imagine rotating their *own* right or left hands into alignment with it. Accordingly, their reaction times increased with increasing amounts of rotation that were required to accomplish this. (See also the study by Cooper and Shepard 1975 on imagining rotations of hands, described in section 4.1.2.) Their mental rotation rates also depended, however, on how *easily* their hands could have been manually turned to achieve these alignments. For example, as illustrated in figure 4.9, an imagined rotation in which the right hand could be pivoted naturally about the wrist was easier to perform than one involving the same amount of rotation but an awkward, unnatural turn of the hand. Similar results were obtained for imagined rotations of other parts of the body, such as the feet. Parsons's findings imply that mental transformations incorporate the natural restrictions on degrees of freedom of bodily motions.

4.5 Representational Momentum in Imagined Transformations

If the principle of transformational equivalence is valid, then one might expect that the *inertial* properties of moving bodies would also be incorporated into imagined transformations. According to the laws of physics, the momentum acquired by a moving object resists any attempt to alter its motion. This is the reason, for example, why a bicycle wheel continues to rotate for some time after one first applies the brakes. Would *imagined* motions also acquire a kind of "momentum," making them hard to stop? And if so, would this internal or "representational" momentum obey the same laws as actual, physical momentum?

Mental rotations, for example, exhibit a kind of "ballistic" quality; they seem to be carried out automatically once initiated (Corballis 1986). Note, however, that evidence for representational momentum

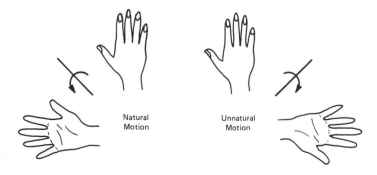

Figure 4.9
Illustration of the relative difficulty in imagining rotations of the hand corresponding to natural motions of the hand about the wrist (left), and awkward, unnatural motions (right). (from Parsons 1987b)

would be hard to obtain using the traditional methods of mental rotation experiments. For instance, if an imagined rotation acquired a kind of inertia, it might overshoot the final orientations slightly, but this would show up only as a small, overall increase in reaction time. Such effects would be hard to distinguish from those having to do with changes in the way the stimuli were encoded or compared. Other methods are therefore needed to demonstrate the existence of representational momentum.

4.5.1 Shifts in Visual Memory Induced by Implied Motions

Jennifer Freyd and I have developed techniques for demonstrating that imagined transformations can indeed exhibit inertial properties. In our first study (Freyd and Finke 1984b), subjects were shown a sequence of three successive views of a rectangle, depicting a rotation of the rectangle at a constant velocity (see figure 4.10). The subjects were told to remember the pattern's final position in the sequence. They were then shown a test pattern, which was either identical to the final pattern or differed from it by a small rotation in the same or opposite direction as the rotation implied by the preceding sequence of views. We predicted that the subjects would find it harder to reject the forward-rotated distractors as being different from the final pattern than the backward-rotated distractors, because the presentation sequence would induce imagined forward continuations of the implied rotation. If this tendency could not be abruptly halted at the pattern's final position, memories of that position would be shifted forward, in analogy to the forward "stopping" distance that results when one tries to stop a physically moving object.

In support of this prediction, the subjects made a substantially greater number of errors in rejecting the forward-rotated distractors,

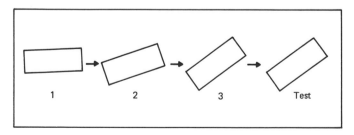

Figure 4.10
Example of trial sequences used in experiments on representational momentum. Subjects were shown three consecutive displays depicting the rotation of a rectangle at a constant rate. They were to compare the final position in the sequence to that of a subsequently presented test pattern. (from Freyd and Finke 1984b)

as shown in figure 4.11. This effect cannot easily be explained in terms of task demands, because the subjects were highly motivated to retain an accurate memory for the pattern's final position. The memory shifts were entirely eliminated, however, in a control condition in which the first two positions in the inducing sequence were reversed, "breaking up" the continuity of the implied rotation.

Supporting evidence for the existence of representational momentum was obtained using inducing displays that implied consistently changing dot patterns (Finke and Freyd 1985). In these more complex displays, the individual dots in the patterns were depicted as moving in separate but consistent directions. As before, forward-shifted distractors were much harder to reject, even though in this case changes in position among the dots were all relative, and hence should have been easier to detect. In addition, these memory shifts were obtained even when the "off" time between the inducing displays was increased well beyond the points where the displays could produce any actual sensations of motion, showing that they were not due to motion aftereffects or other types of sensory artifacts (Anstis and Moulden 1970; Cavanaugh and Favreau 1980).

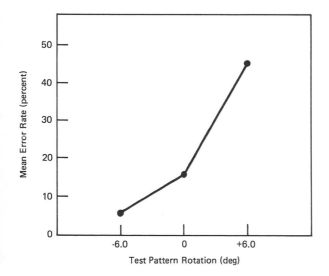

Figure 4.11
Mean error rate for judging whether the test pattern was in the same orientation as the final pattern in the implied rotation sequence, depending on whether the test pattern was aligned with the final pattern or was rotated forward or backward from it. The larger error rate for judging the forward-rotated test pattern suggests that the subjects' memories of the final orientation had been shifted forward (from Freyd and Finke 1984b)

4.5.2 Velocity Dependence of the Memory Shifts

Physical momentum increases as an object's velocity increases, and the same is true of representational momentum. Freyd and I modified the procedures in our first study to vary the implied velocity of the inducing motions and to measure the magnitude of the memory shifts (Freyd and Finke 1985). Implied velocity was manipulated by varying the time between consecutive presentations of the inducing stimuli, and the memory shifts were estimated by using a range of distractor displacements, distributed about the actual final position. The probability that the subjects judged each distractor as being identical to the remembered pattern permitted us to construct probability distributions, the peaks of which provided estimates of how far the memories had been shifted forward (see figure 4.12). As shown in figure 4.13, the estimated memory shifts increased in direct proportion to the implied velocity of the inducing sequence.

This velocity dependence of the memory shifts was extended by Finke, Freyd, and Shyi (1986) to cases where the inducing sequence implied a consistent *change* in velocity. For a real, moving object, the

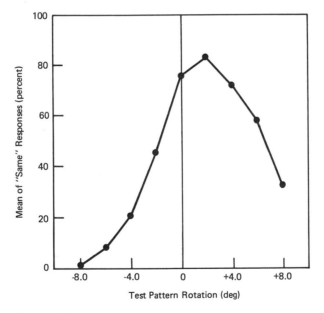

Figure 4.12
Mean percentages of "same" responses given to test patterns that were rotated by varying amounts from the final orientation of a pattern that had been depicted as moving at one of nine velocities. The peak of the resulting distribution provided an estimate of the size of the forward memory shift. (from Freyd and Finke 1985)

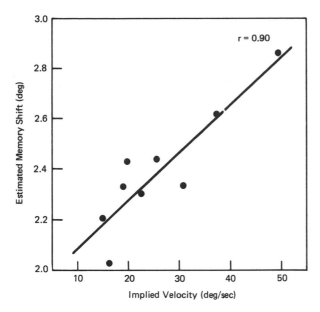

Figure 4.13
Estimated memory shift with changes in the implied velocity. The increasing linear function suggests that representational momentum, like physical momentum, increases as the velocity increases. (from Freyd and Finke 1985)

momentum that the object acquires depends on its final velocity, not on how that final velocity was achieved. This, too, appears to be a characteristic of representational momentum. Subjects were shown inducing sequences implying that objects were moving at a constant velocity, a constant acceleration, or a constant deceleration, where the average implied velocities were equated. In each case, the memory shifts were determined by the final velocities implied at the end of the sequence. In particular, when the inducing sequence implied a deceleration to a final velocity of zero (where, by analogy, there would be no physical momentum), the memory shifts were eliminated.

Representational momentum, like physical momentum, thus depends on the final velocity. In Finke, Freyd, and Shyi (1986) we proposed a theory to explain this velocity dependence. According to our theory, the implied motions are initially extrapolated forward from the final position in the sequence, at the rate depicted by the inducing displays. This tendency must be resisted if the final position is to be remembered accurately. However, because the imagined motions have acquired representational momentum, the extrapolation process cannot be instantly halted at this final position. This results in small, forward memory shifts. Further, because the amount of representational momentum increases with increases in the rate at which the implied motions are mentally extrapolated, the shifts in memory for final position increase with increases in the implied velocity. If, for some reason, the extrapolation process is disrupted, as when the inducing displays imply motions that are inconsistent, there will be no representational momentum, and no memory shifts.

These findings are not susceptible to many of the criticisms that have been made of other kinds of imagery and mental rotation experiments. As already mentioned, the requirements of the task discourage subjects from trying to mentally simulate continuations of the implied motions. Experimenter bias is also an unlikely explanation, because the experimenters in these studies encouraged accurate performance, and they were never in contact with the subjects during the testing procedures. Because the displays were presented sequentially, often at very slow rates, eye movements could not have explained the memory shifts (cf. section 4.3.3). Finally, the linear dependence of the memory shifts on implied velocity would seem to rule out any simple explanation in terms of descriptions or propositional representations of the remembered patterns.

4.5.3 Measuring Rates of Mental Extrapolation

More recently, Gary Shyi and I have compared performance in the memory task with that in which the subjects were specifically told to imagine continuations of the implied motions all the way forward to the next step in the inducing sequence (Finke and Shyi 1988). We wanted to see whether there was a general tendency to "overshoot" in carrying out the mental extrapolations. Our theory predicts that forward-shifted errors should only occur when one has to *resist* the extrapolation process. If the implied motions were imagined to continue at their proper rate, judgments of the future positions would normally be accurate (Jagacinski, Johnson, and Miller 1983; Rosenbaum 1975). But if the extrapolation process breaks down or slows up at some point, then the extrapolation errors should be shifted backward with respect to the correct positions. These predictions were supported by the results of this study. When subjects tried to extrapolate the implied motions to the next step in the inducing sequence, their errors increased as the implied velocity increased and were shifted backward, suggesting that their extrapolations had fallen short of the correct positions. In contrast, their memory shifts for these same implied motions were in the forward direction. This implies that the memory shifts obtained in experiments on representational momentum cannot be attributed to a general tendency to overshoot when mentally extrapolating the implied motions.

4.5.4 Generalizations and Limitations of Representational Momentum

Mike Kelly and Jennifer Freyd (1987) have explored whether representational momentum can also be created using other kinds of implied transformations. In one of their experiments, the inducing sequence depicted a square growing larger or smaller, implying motion toward or away from the observer in depth. Memories for the final size of the square were shifted forward in depth in the direction of the implied motion. In another experiment, the inducing sequence depicted a rectangle changing its shape in a consistent way into another rectangle. Memories for the final shape in the sequence were again shifted forward in the direction of the implied change. Kelly and Freyd also investigated whether representational momentum could occur in nonvisual modalities. They presented subjects with a sequence of tones that either increased or decreased in pitch at a constant rate. Memories for the pitch of the last-heard tone were shifted in the direction of the implied changes in pitch. Thus, representational momentum is not restricted only to imagined motions of rigid, physical objects, but may be extended to other types of mental transformations that can be carried out in a consistent and predictable way (see also section 4.2.4).

There are other differences between representational momentum and physical momentum. For instance, Kelly and Freyd (1987) found that when an implied change in shape ended with the final form being a highly familiar and regular shape (such as a rectangle being transformed into a square), there was little evidence for any shift in memory for the final form. Finke and Shyi (1988) found that the memory shifts were larger when the direction of mental extrapolation was always the same on every trial than when it was varied unpredictably from trial to trial. Physical momentum, of course, does not depend on the familiarity of an object or on how consistently a particular motion has been repeated in the past. These constitute exceptions to the principle of transformational equivalence. It also remains to be seen whether the memory shifts are affected by changes in the implied *mass* of the objects, which one would expect from a strict analogy to physical momentum.

4.5.5 The Time Course of the Memory Shifts

A final issue to be considered is the manner in which the memory shifts grow during the initial part of the retention interval. If imagined transformations, like physical transformations, are carried out

in a continuous fashion, the memory shifts should at first increase
at a constant rate and should then level off to a maximum point once
the imagined transformation has been effectively stopped. This was
shown by Freyd and Johnson (1987). They probed the time course
of the memory shifts for extremely short retention intervals ranging
from 10 to 90 milliseconds, using inducing sequences that depicted
a rotating rectangle, similar to that presented in figure 4.10. As shown
in figure 4.14, the memory shifts increased by fractional amounts in
proportion to these small increments in the retention period. At
longer retention intervals, the memory shifts continued to grow, but
at an increasingly slower rate, reaching a maximum forward shift at
around 300 milliseconds.

The findings of Freyd and Johnson offer the strongest evidence to
date for the continuity of mentally extrapolated motions. Whereas
experiments on mental rotation have demonstrated that imagined
rotations are approximately continuous, down to a resolution of
about 30 degrees (Cooper 1976a; see section 4.2.2), the Freyd and
Johnson findings reveal that imagined rotations are continuous *down
to a fraction of a degree* (see again figure 4.14). Such findings are clearly
inconsistent with proposals that the imagined motions are carried
out only in a discrete, stepwise manner (e.g., Just and Carpenter
1985). Moreover, it is exceedingly unlikely that these findings can be

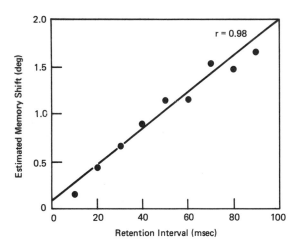

Figure 4.14
Estimated memory shift as the retention interval increased. The constant growth in
the memory shifts during these short retention intervals (less than 100 msec) suggests
that imagined extrapolations of the implied rotations were carried out continuously.
(from Freyd and Johnson 1987)

explained in terms of deliberate simulations based on tacit knowledge about the effects of momentum, given that the memory shifts are instantiated so rapidly. Rather, they appear to reflect the inherent inertial and analog properties of the imagined transformations.

4.6 Summary and Conclusions

Like actual physical transformations, imagined transformations appear to be holistic and continuous and to exhibit inertial characteristics. These findings support the principle of transformational equivalence. In addition, imagined transformations correspond to a wide variety of physical transformations, including those involving changes in size, color, shape, and auditory pitch. They also incorporate the internal, biomechanical constraints on actual bodily movements. Exceptions to the principle do exist, however, and are often found when a mental transformation has been insufficiently practiced or when alternative strategies exist for judging stimuli.

4.7 Further Explorations

4.7.1 Recommendations for Further Reading
Extensive reviews of studies on mental rotation can be found in book chapters by Cooper and Shepard (1973a, 1978), Shepard (1975), Shepard and Podgorny (1978), Metzler and Shepard (1974), and Finke and Shepard (1986). Shepard and Cooper's *Mental Images and Their Transformations* (1982) brings together original reports of many of their studies discussed in this chapter. Less technical articles by Shepard (1978b) and by Cooper and Shepard (1984) are also of interest. For recent evidence that animals can also perform mental rotations, see Neiworth and Rilling (1987).

Further discussions of experiments on representational momentum and their implications can be found in articles by Finke, Freyd, and Shyi (1986), Kelly and Freyd (1987), and Freyd (1987). Freyd has reviewed these and other studies demonstrating that many types of mental representations are intrinsically dynamic. For instance, she has found that memory shifts extending forward in time also occur when subjects are shown photographs taken during the middle of familiar action sequences (Freyd 1983b), or are shown displays in which objects previously at rest suddenly become unsupported (Freyd, Pantzer, and Cheng, in press). Her work has also shown that knowledge about the motions used to construct recognizable patterns, such as handwritten characters, can lead to distortions in memory that are consistent with those motions (Babcock and Freyd, in press; Freyd 1983c).

4.7.2 Similarities Between Mental Transformations and Apparent Motion

Additional studies by Shepard and his colleagues have shown that *visual apparent motion*, an illusory motion created when patterns differing in position or orientation are presented in rapid alternation (Kolers 1972), is similar in many respects to mental rotation and related types of mental transformations. For instance, there exists a linear relation between presentation time and separation distance for producing optimal sensations of apparent motion (Shepard and Judd 1976; Shepard and Zare 1983). Apparent motions also seem to pass through all the intermediate points along the implied trajectory (Robins and Shepard 1977; see also Freyd 1983a). Apparent transformations in shape have also been demonstrated; these, too, depend on the rate at which the inducing patterns are presented (Farrell and Shepard 1981; Kolers and Pomerantz 1971). These findings suggest that similar kinds of internal mechanisms might underlie perceived and imagined motions, consistent with the principle of perceptual equivalence, which was considered in chapter 2.

4.7.3 Individual Differences in Mental Rotation

It is difficult to evaluate reported differences among individual rates of mental rotation, because subjects who show faster rates also tend to be faster at encoding and comparing the presented stimuli (Cooper and Regan 1982). Such differences may simply reflect overall differences in spatial ability (McGee 1979), rather than differences in the ability to carry out, specifically, an imagined rotation. There is also evidence that subjects having high and low spatial ability make different kinds of eye movements in mental rotation tasks (Just and Carpenter 1985), making it hard to interpret reported differences in mental rotation rate when eye movements were not controlled. Further complicating this situation is evidence from Cooper (1976b) that subjects also differ in the kinds of strategies they use for comparing the patterns, once they complete the mental rotations (see also Cooper and Podgorny 1976).

4.7.4 Predicting the Trajectories of Extrapolated Motions

The findings on representational momentum presented in section 4.5 appear to conflict with those of studies that have investigated what people seem to know about the natural motions of objects. McCloskey and Kohl (1983) have reported, for example, that people often have erroneous beliefs about the way objects will continue to move once forces constraining the objects are removed. For instance, people tend to think that when a ball emerges from a curved tube, it will continue to move in a slightly curved path, in the absence of any other forces. (According to the principle of inertia, the ball would actually move in a straight line once it emerged from the tube.) How can these findings be reconciled with those suggesting that imagined motions exhibit the inertial properties of actual physical motions?

Kaiser, Proffitt, and Anderson (1985) have reported that people are much better at predicting the correct trajectories of objects when they are actually shown various possible motions and are asked to pick out the correct one, than when they attempt to solve the problem in a purely "conceptual" way. This suggests that people may have tacit knowledge about the proper trajectories of objects that isn't available to ordinary retrieval processes (see again Pylyshyn 1981 and the relevant discussions of tacit knowledge in sections 2.2.5 and 3.2.2). Also, as my colleagues and I have proposed (Finke, Freyd, and Shyi 1986), *which* representational pathway is used when imagining continuations of a motion is a separate issue from whether or not representational momentum will be created, once the pathway is selected. Whereas the former may indeed depend on factors such as tacit knowledge and task demands, the latter seems not to.

Chapter 5

Mental Constructions and Discoveries

Little has been said so far about how the parts of an image are put together and whether images can be reorganized or reinterpreted, once assembled. A person's introspections, for instance, suggest that images can often be constructed and interpreted in highly original ways. For example, can you imagine an animal having the body of a lion and the legs of an ostrich? What would this mythical animal look like? How would it walk? What does it remind you of? The present chapter will consider scientific studies that have explored the structures that emerge when images are formed, and whether people can actually make new "discoveries" by mentally inspecting these structures. These issues will be addressed, first of all, by considering how well people can mentally synthesize particular kinds of objects or patterns from a given set of parts.

5.1 Demonstrations of Mental Synthesis

Mental synthesis has usually been studied in one of two ways: by presenting the parts of an object separately and by designating the parts by verbal labels or descriptions.

5.1.1 Mentally Assembling the Parts of Patterns

Thompson and Klatzky (1978) demonstrated that people can mentally fuse the separately presented parts of a pattern in order to verify whether or not the synthesized pattern matches one that is presented intact. They were interested in seeing whether the parts would be completely integrated in the mentally synthesized forms. Thompson and Klatzky predicted that this would be true when the parts could be mentally assembled to make a familiar, closed form, where the parts would blend together naturally, but not when the parts made a form that was poorly organized, where the parts would more likely retain their individual identities. To use an analogy, one can assemble the pieces of a puzzle so that the pieces fit together well and blend together, or so that they fit poorly, allowing the original pieces to stand out.

The subjects in the Thompson and Klatzky study were shown drawings, such as those in figure 5.1, that consisted either of a single, intact pattern, or of the spatially separated pieces of a pattern. Their task was to mentally fuse the separate drawings to make a whole pattern, and then, after they had completed their mental synthesis, to verify whether that pattern was identical to one that was presented subsequently. Thompson and Klatzky varied both the number of drawings to be mentally synthesized (from 1 to 3) and whether or not the parts of the synthesized pattern could be combined to make a familiar, closed geometric form. The time it took the subjects to verify that the second pattern corresponded to the synthesized pattern is presented in figure 5.2. Although their response times increased with increasing number of components, this effect was much smaller when the parts could be easily integrated, suggesting that the subjects were at least partly successful at achieving a complete mental synthesis.

5.1.2 Verifying Objects from Their Descriptions
People can also imagine how something looks from a description of its parts and then compare the imagined form to one that is actually presented. To take one example, Nielsen and Smith (1973) gave subjects descriptions of the features of faces, which they then com-

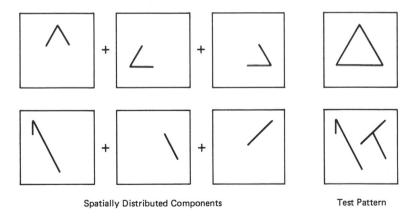

Spatially Distributed Components   Test Pattern

Figure 5.1
Examples of stimuli used in experiments on mental synthesis. Subjects were instructed to mentally fuse the spatially distributed parts to make a complete pattern, and then to verify whether that pattern matched a test pattern that was presented shortly thereafter. (from Thompson and Klatzky 1978)

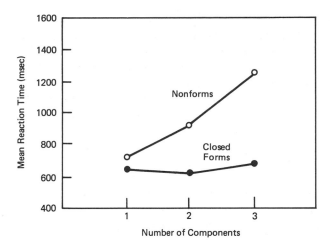

Figure 5.2
Mean reaction time to verify that the mentally synthesized pattern matched the test pattern as the number of components in the mental synthesis increased, and depending on whether or not the pattern corresponded to a familiar, closed form. The different slopes of the reaction time functions suggest that the subjects were more successful at achieving a complete mental synthesis when the parts could be combined to make a familiar pattern. (from Thompson and Klatzky 1978)

pared with drawings of the faces. The number of features was varied, as was the amount of preparation time before the drawings of the faces were shown. Nielsen and Smith found that, as the preparation time increased, the number of features had less effect on the time it took to verify the descriptions. Presumably this was because the subjects were then able to form mental images of the faces, integrating the described features. Similarly, Intons-Peterson (1981) found that verification time for recognizing faces from descriptions was independent of the number of features when the features were arranged on the faces in a natural way but not when the features were in an unnatural arrangement (for example, with the eyes, nose, and mouth in scrambled positions). Again, this suggests that it is much easier to achieve a complete mental synthesis when the parts form a natural or familiar unit.

When designating parts of objects by descriptions, one always needs to consider the possibility that subjects might simply rely on those descriptions in recognizing the presented forms, without forming images of them. (The issue of how to distinguish images from descriptions was also considered in section 1.3.) For example, Clark and Chase (1972) had subjects verify whether or not descriptions of the relative positions of a "star" and "plus" symbol corresponded to their actual relative positions in a visual display. They found that the verification times depended on the way the relative positions were described ("The star is above the plus" vs. "The star is not below the plus"), suggesting that the subjects had performed the task by remembering the descriptions, as opposed to forming images of the symbols. Whether images or descriptions are used in verifying descriptions of objects may depend, however, on whether subjects are given an adequate opportunity to form the image. Barbara Tversky (1975) found, in a similar task comparing sentences and pictures, that the linguistic form of the descriptions mattered when the descriptions were presented simultaneously with the pictures, but not when the pictures were presented 5 seconds after the descriptions. Similar findings were also reported by Seymour (1974).

5.2 The Principle of Structural Equivalence

These studies indicate that mental images are often useful in preparing one to recognize an object from a description or presentation of its parts or features. (See also the related discussion of the "perceptual anticipation" hypothesis in section 2.4.1). If indeed parts of an object can be "fused" together in a mental image, then an image may have certain *structural* properties in common with actual physical objects. If so, it may then be possible to detect *emergent* structures in an image that may not have been anticipated at the time the image was formed.

Our final principle, the principle of *structural equivalence*, makes a general proposal about the structural characteristics of mental images:

The structure of mental images corresponds to that of actual perceived objects, in the sense that the structure is coherent, well organized, and can be reorganized and reinterpreted.

Note that this principle is distinct from the principle of perceptual equivalence (discussed in chapter 2), or that of spatial equivalence (discussed in chapter 3), because an image could exhibit many of the perceptual and spatial characteristics of objects without exhibiting any of their structural characteristics. For example, an image might have constraints on visual resolution, yield perceptual aftereffects, have spatially distributed parts, and so on, without depicting any of the structural relationships among the parts that would be inherent in an actual object. Further, even if an image did appear to "resemble" an actual object, it might not be reinterpretable as anything else. Physical objects, in contrast, can often be reinterpreted.

5.2.1 Mental Constructions of Geometric Patterns

The principle of structural equivalence has been supported by studies showing that structural relationships among the parts of complex geometric patterns can be preserved in mental images. Glushko and Cooper (1978) undertook an investigation of the various factors that influence whether or not parts of imagined patterns are completely assembled in an image. Subjects were presented with descriptions of forms that were constructed by juxtaposing familiar geometric shapes, or they were actually shown the completed forms (see figure 5.3). Their task was to compare the described or presented forms to test forms that were presented shortly thereafter. There were two findings of interest. First, as shown in figure 5.4, when the subjects were given as much time as they needed to prepare for the test form, the number of shapes comprising the remembered form had little effect on the time required to verify that the forms matched. Second, the linguistic properties of descriptions of the remembered forms, as well as the number of parts, mattered only when the subjects were given insufficient preparation time. Thus, when the subjects had sufficient time to mentally synthesize the parts, their images preserved the structural characteristics of the actual patterns, regardless of whether the parts had been described or actually shown.

A related study by Murphy and Hutchinson (1982) showed that the structurally distinctive properties of patterns can influence one's

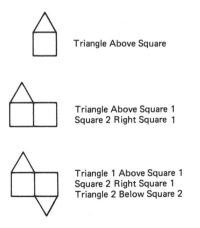

Figure 5.3
Examples of figures and descriptions used in experiments on mentally synthesizing patterns out of geometric parts. Subjects verified whether the pattern or its description matched a subsequently presented test pattern. (from Glushko and Cooper 1978)

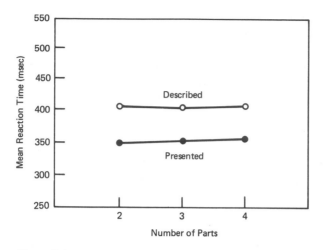

Figure 5.4
Mean reaction time to verify that a pattern or its description matched a test pattern as the number of parts making up the pattern increased. The absence of an effect of the number of parts in each case suggests that the subjects were able to mentally synthesize the entire pattern from its description. (from Glushko and Cooper 1978)

memory for those patterns, whether the patterns are mentally synthesized from descriptions or are seen as a whole. In one condition, the patterns to be remembered were specified verbally using a blank 4 × 4 grid. Each cell in the grid was described as being blank, filled, or diagonally half-filled (see figure 5.5), and the subjects were instructed to visualize the assembled pattern as each of the parts was added. In another condition, the entire pattern was actually presented. Errors in drawing the patterns following a retention interval varied in the same way in each condition with changes in the structural characteristics of the patterns. For example, patterns that were bilaterally symmetrical were remembered more accurately than asymmetrical patterns, regardless of whether the patterns had been mentally synthesized or had actually been shown. Such findings further imply that mental images preserve a pattern's structural characteristics.

5.2.2 Mental Constructions of Three-Dimensional Objects
The principle of structural equivalence also applies to the mental synthesis of three-dimensional forms. Cooper (in press) reported studies in which mechanical engineering students were initially shown two orthographic views of an object followed by a third orthographic view. Their task was to say whether or not the third

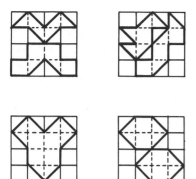

Figure 5.5
Examples of patterns used in experiments on mentally assembling an ongoing sequence of parts. The subjects were told to imagine the parts, one at a time, in appropriate cells of a square grid. Errors in recalling the imagined patterns, like patterns that were actually seen, depended on the global features of the patterns such as their bilateral symmetry. This suggests that the overall structure of a mental image is similar to that of an actual pattern. (from Murphy and Hutchinson 1982)

view was compatible with the first two; that is, whether the three orthographic views would correspond to the same three-dimensional object. After making these judgments for a series of objects, the subjects were then shown *isometric* views of the objects, along with distractors, in a surprise recognition test. They were able to identify correctly over 85 percent of the items from the isometric views, even though they had previously seen only their orthographic projections. To explain these findings, Cooper proposed that the subjects had mentally constructed the three-dimensional structures of the objects, which they then used to verify the compatibility of the flat, orthographic views and to recognize the previously unseen isometric views.

Cooper's findings are consistent with those of Shepard and Metzler (1971), discussed in section 4.1.1, which demonstrated that people could mentally rotate the three-dimensional structure of objects when shown flat, perspective drawings of the objects. More recently, Klopfer (1985) has shown that subjects can mentally synthesize the Shepard-Metzler forms when the forms are presented a section at a time in a series of visual displays. The time it took the subjects to complete their mental constructions depended on the structural complexity of the forms, as opposed to the number of displays depicting the individual sections.

5.2.3 Structural Factors Influencing Image Generation Time

One of the common misconceptions about mental imagery is that images are generated all at once, like a slide being projected onto a viewing screen. On the contrary, the more complex a mental image is—for example, the more parts or items contained in the image—the longer it takes to generate the image (Beech and Allport 1978; Glushko and Cooper 1978; Klopfer 1985; Kosslyn, Cave, Provost, and von Gierke, in press; Morris and Reid 1973; Roth and Kosslyn, in press). In addition, because larger images usually contain more information about the detailed parts of an object, it also takes longer to generate a large image (that is, one that subtends a large visual angle) than a small image (Farah and Kosslyn 1981; Kosslyn 1975). These findings suggest that mental images are assembled in parts, as opposed to being generated with the parts already assembled.

The most extensive study to date on the factors that influence image generation time was carried out by Kosslyn, Reiser, Farah, and Fliegel (1983). In their first two experiments, they verified that increasing the number of parts in an object increases the time it takes to visualize the object. Their third experiment, however, was particularly relevant to the issue of structural equivalence. The subjects were shown drawings of patterns that were constructed out of simple geometric forms (see figure 5.6), after being given descriptions of the patterns. These patterns were described in one of two ways, either in terms of a large number of small, juxtaposed parts, or in terms of

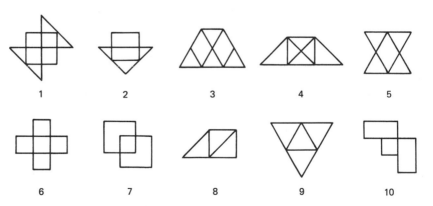

Figure 5.6
Stimuli used in experiments on whether the number of parts specified in descriptions of a pattern influences the time it takes to generate an image of the pattern. Each of the above patterns could be described either in terms of many small, juxtaposed parts, or in terms of a few large, overlapping parts. (from Kosslyn, Reiser, Farah, and Fliegel 1983)

a small number of large, overlapping parts. For example, drawing 6 in figure 5.6 was described as being composed of "five squares" in one condition and "two overlapping rectangles" in another. Hence, the number of parts, as specified by the descriptions, could vary within patterns that were *physically identical*. The subjects were instructed to generate an image of the patterns according to the descriptions, and their generation times were recorded. To ensure that they would include all of the parts in their images, the subjects were questioned about the presence of a particular geometric form in the patterns, or about the presence of a particular axis of symmetry.

As shown in figure 5.7, the time needed to generate the images increased in proportion to the number of parts that were designated in the descriptions, even for the physically identical patterns. This finding suggests that mental images are constructed according to how one initially conceives of the structure of an object. Just as it takes more time to construct a physical object that has more parts, so, too, does it take more time to mentally "assemble" the parts of an image as the number of parts increases. This also reinforces the

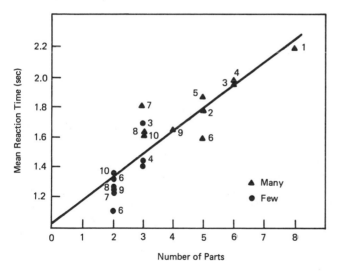

Figure 5.7
Mean reaction time to generate images of the patterns shown in figure 5.6, according to the number of parts mentioned in descriptions of the patterns. Reaction times for imagining physically identical patterns are distinguished by whether they were described in terms of many or few parts. The linear dependence of image generation time on the number of parts suggests that images are formed on the basis of how one initially conceives of the component structure of an object or pattern. (from Kosslyn, Reiser, Farah, and Fliegel 1983)

argument, presented in section 1.5.3, that mental images are not truly like "photographs" of objects, because structural descriptions of objects clearly influence the way an image is formed.

Kosslyn et al. conducted a fourth experiment that also bears on whether mental images are structurally equivalent to physical objects. Over fifty years ago, the Gestalt psychologists had identified the major principles by which one organizes perceived objects into meaningful units and groupings (Koffka 1935; Kohler 1947). For example, objects that are physically nearer to one another are seen as belonging together; this is the *law of proximity*. Similarly, objects that lie along a continuous path are also seen as belonging together; this is the *law of good continuation*. Kosslyn et al. had subjects generate images of letter arrays containing the same number of letters, but varying in the number of groupings of the letters, as defined by these Gestalt principles. As predicted, the image generation times were longer when the letters made up a larger number of Gestalt units. For example, it took longer to generate an image consisting of four columns of three letters each than an image consisting of two columns of six letters each. These findings, therefore, imply that mental images are interpreted according to the same kinds of organizing principles as physically observed objects.

5.3 Criticisms of Experiments on Imagined Constructions

I have been arguing that mental images are formed according to the same kinds of structures as one perceives in actual physical objects. However, if the principle of structural equivalence is valid, it should also be possible to *reinterpret* the structure of a mental image after it is formed, just as it is often possible to reinterpret the structure of a perceived object or pattern. Many types of patterns, for instance, are inherently ambiguous and can be interpreted perceptually in many different ways (Attneave 1971; Shepard and Cermak 1973). For example, the pattern shown in figure 5.8, taken from Shepard and Cermak (1973), can be seen as a jet, a seashell, or the head of a

Figure 5.8
Example of multiple interpretations (four images on right) of a perceptually ambiguous pattern (left-most image), generated by a polar coordinate analog to Fourier synthesis. (from Shepard and Cermak 1973)

chicken. The same should be true of mental images of patterns. However, the studies to be considered next have reported striking failures to demonstrate the reinterpretability of mental images, calling the principle of structural equivalence into question.

5.3.1 Failure to Detect Structurally Inferior Parts in Mental Images

If mental images do preserve structural ambiguities, then one should be able to detect parts in an image that are not apparent in the initial structural description of the object. That this can be very difficult was demonstrated by Stephen Reed (1974). His subjects were shown a pattern to memorize; this was followed by a test pattern that either did or did not constitute a possible part of the memorized pattern. The "goodness" of the parts was varied according to whether or not the parts would have been contained in an initial structural description of the pattern (see figure 5.9). For example, the first pattern in figure 5.9 would naturally be described as "two overlapping triangles" or "two adjacent hourglasses" but not as "two overlapping parallelograms." Reed found that subjects could rarely detect any of the structurally inferior parts in their images of the patterns. In contrast, when the parts were shown first, followed by the entire pattern, subjects could easily tell that the structurally inferior parts were contained in the patterns (Reed and Johnsen 1975). In the latter case, having the patterns actually present during the decision process made it possible to detect the "hidden" parts. (See also the related

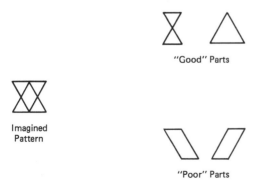

Figure 5.9
Examples of failures to detect structurally inferior parts in imagined patterns. Subjects were initially shown a whole pattern to remember (left) and were then asked to say whether various parts were contained in the remembered pattern (right). The subjects could perform the task successfully only when the parts were structurally "good" parts; i.e., when they would have been mentioned in a description of the pattern. (from Reed 1974)

findings on detecting structurally inferior parts in mentally rotated patterns discussed in section 4.3.1.)

A similar demonstration of how the "goodness" of parts can affect one's ability to detect the parts in an image was reported by Stephen Palmer (1977). His subjects were instructed to mentally synthesize patterns that were composed of various "units," consisting of combinations of horizontal, vertical, or diagonal lines. Ratings were obtained for the goodness of each unit in each pattern. As in Reed's study, the subjects had difficulty verifying the presence of the structurally inferior units in the mentally synthesized patterns. Palmer found, specifically, that the time required to verify that the units were contained in the patterns decreased as the rated goodness of the units increased. Again, such findings suggest that it is not easy to restructure the parts of an image.

Additional evidence that certain kinds of structures are difficult to detect in mental images was provided by Geoffrey Hinton (1979). He offers the following demonstration. Imagine that a solid cube is turned such that one of its corners is pointing directly at you. How many other corners of the cube can you now "see" in your image? Hinton found that most people erroneously report that they can mentally "see" four other corners, whereas the correct answer is actually *six*. This suggests that people do not represent the entire three-dimensional structure of objects in their mental images. Instead, they rely on structural descriptions that may be incomplete or misleading—for example, that a cube is supposed to have a total of six corners rather than eight.

5.3.2 Failure to Detect Perceptual Reversals in Mental Images of Ambiguous Figures

An even more serious challenge to the principle of structural equivalence comes from a study by Chambers and Reisberg (1985). In their experiments, subjects were shown classic ambiguous figures, such as the "duck/rabbit" and "Necker cube," for brief inspection periods. These figures, when viewed continuously, exhibit dramatic perceptual reversals (see figure 5.10). Chambers and Reisberg wanted to find out whether it was also possible to detect these same reversals in mental images of the figures. After briefly inspecting the patterns, the subjects were instructed to close their eyes and to form mental images of them, and to report any reversals they might experience. Although they were previously trained in detecting reversals when looking at similar types of figures, they never once reported the correct reversals in their images. Yet, when the subjects were later asked to draw the patterns from memory, and to inspect their draw-

 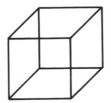

Figure 5.10
Examples of perceptually reversible figures used in experiments on reinterpreting mental images. The figure on the left is known as the "duck-rabbit" and the figure on the right as the "Necker cube." The subjects were shown the figures briefly and then tried to detect perceptual reversals of the figures in their imagery. They were never able to do so. (from Chambers and Reisberg 1985)

ings, they *were* able to detect the correct reversals. Chambers and Reisberg concluded, therefore, that mental images cannot be reinterpreted or reconstrued, because an image, unlike a visually perceived object or picture, always corresponds to a single, initial interpretation or description.

Jerry Fodor (1975) has argued that mental images are capable of representing things because they are interpreted entities, not because they "resemble" objects. That is to say, mental images, unlike pictures, do not exist in an uninterpreted form. To use one of his examples, a mental image of a pregnant woman is inherently different from an image of an overweight woman, because the imager would always know which type of woman the image refers to (see also Shepard 1978b). Pictures of these same women, in contrast, could be completely ambiguous as to whether the women were pregnant or overweight. Chambers and Reisberg extended this argument to conclude that because an image must be tied to some initial interpretation, it cannot be reinterpreted as representing something else. As will be shown, however, this is strictly an empirical question. The next section, in fact, will examine evidence that mental images *can* be reinterpreted.

5.4 Recognizing Emergent Patterns in Mental Images

Even if it is very difficult, or even impossible, to detect perceptual reversals or structurally inferior parts in images, it might still be possible to reinterpret the structure of an image in other ways. In particular, it might be possible to detect novel, unexpected structures following certain types of mental constructions or transformations, especially if the image is not too strongly tied to an initial interpretation.

5.4.1 Detecting Novel Structures in Mental Images

It is well known that the identity of an object can sometimes change if the object is rotated (Rock 1973). This also seems to be true of mental images. Shepard and Feng (reported in Shepard and Cooper 1982) found that subjects could identify letters resulting from the imagined rotation or reflection of another letter. For example, when instructed to imagine rotating the letter N by 90 degrees, most subjects reported detecting the letter Z. In experiments reported by Slee (1980), subjects were first shown patterns similar to those used in the Reed (1974) study (see again figure 5.9), were then shown "good" or "poor" parts of the patterns, and were asked to draw the patterns from memory, starting with the presented part. The subjects could perform this task almost as well with the structurally poor parts as with the structurally good parts. Hollins (1985) had subjects imagine filling in squares of a grid, designated by verbal coordinates, to form patterns resembling recognizable objects such as a car and a telephone. The subjects were able to identify the resulting pattern in their images on about half the trials.

These findings suggest that subjects can sometimes reinterpret an imagined pattern or recognize structures that emerge when parts of the pattern are mentally assembled. However, they do not entirely rule out alternative explanations, such as guessing strategies. For example, a person might figure out what letter corresponds to a rotated N, without having to rely on mental imagery, by merely thinking about what kinds of letters might contain the rotated parts.

5.4.2 Emergent Patterns in Imagined Rotations of Three-Dimensional Arrays

Steven Pinker and I have carried out experiments to explore the recognition of unexpected patterns in mentally rotated displays (Pinker and Finke 1980). Recall from chapter 3 that Pinker (1980) had found that subjects could imagine scanning a three-dimensional array of objects either in depth or across a two-dimensional "projection" of the objects as seen from particular vantage points (see section 3.1.2). We wondered whether people would also be able to recognize familiar patterns, made up of configurations of the objects, that would "emerge" with imagined changes in viewing perspective. An analogy would be the way constellations form recognizable patterns as seen from the earth. These constellations would be entirely different if observed from a planet in a different star system; they are thus specific to one's vantage point in space.

Using methods similar to those of Pinker (1980), we began by having subjects learn the locations of four small toys suspended inside a clear plastic cylinder. After the objects were removed, the cylinder was rotated 90 degrees, and the subjects were instructed to imagine that the objects had rotated along with the cylinder. They were then asked whether they could recognize the shape formed by the objects by mentally "looking" at them from this new vantage point. Nearly half the subjects reported that they could recognize a tilted parallelogram, which was the shape that the objects would have formed had they actually been seen from the rotated perspective. However, none of the subjects were able to guess, prior to the mental rotation, what the emergent shape would be. Thus, it is unlikely that they could have based their responses on descriptions of the objects or other analytical strategies. Rather, the three-dimensional structure of the arrays must have been preserved in the rotated images, independent of how that structure was described or interpreted initially.

5.4.3 Unanticipated Discoveries in Imagined Visual Constructions

Pinker, Martha Farah, and I recently conducted a set of experiments to determine how likely it is that subjects could detect emergent patterns in an image and then reinterpret what the image represents (Finke, Pinker, and Farah, in press). In our first experiment, the subjects were instructed to mentally superimpose two familiar patterns, consisting of alphanumeric characters or simple geometric forms. They were to report any new shapes that emerged from their imagined synthesis; these shapes could consist of either geometric or "symbolic" forms. An example would be the following: Imagine the capital letter H. Now imagine placing the capital letter X directly over it, such that the four corners of each letter coincide. What new forms can you now detect? Subjects in the experiment reported a variety of emergent forms for this pattern combination, such as geometric shapes (right triangles), other letters (N, M, and a rotated Z), and recognizable objects (a "butterfly" and a "bow tie"). Similar results were obtained for other pattern combinations, examples of which are shown in figure 5.11.

Of course, some of these emergent forms might have been guessed simply from knowing what the initial patterns were. Also, few of the emergent shapes constituted reinterpretations of the *entire* synthesized pattern. To overcome these limitations, we conducted additional experiments in which subjects were instructed to begin with a starting pattern, then to imagine transforming the pattern in specified ways, and finally to report what the resulting pattern looked like. For example, imagine the capital letter B. Now rotate the B 90 degrees to the left. Put a triangle directly below it having the same width

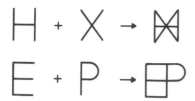

Figure 5.11
Examples of mentally synthesized patterns in experiments on detecting emergent forms in images. All of the subjects were able to detect at least one emergent form in their imagined constructions. (from Finke, Pinker, and Farah, in press)

and pointing down. Remove the horizontal line. Can you recognize the resulting pattern? The correct emergent pattern would be a "heart." Using these kinds of transformation sequences, examples of which are shown in figure 5.12, subjects were able to recognize the resulting pattern on about half of the trials. Moreover, their success depended on how accurately they had carried out the transformations. When the transformations had been correctly performed, as assessed by the subjects' drawings at the end of each trial, the final pattern was recognized about two-thirds of the time. However, when the transformations had been performed incorrectly, the final pattern was *never* recognized. This argues against their having used strategies based solely on their knowledge about the starting pattern and the descriptions of the transformation sequence.

We then ran another experiment to rule out the possibility that subjects could guess the emerging pattern at some point before the imagined transformation was complete. The procedure was similar to that used in the previous experiment, except that now the subjects were explicitly asked to guess, at each step in the transformation sequence, what the final, resulting pattern was likely to be. For example, imagine the capital letter F. Guess what the final pattern will be. Connect a lower-case letter b to the vertical line in the F. Guess what the final pattern will be. Now flip the loop of the b around so that it's now on the left side of the vertical line. Can you recognize this pattern? In the actual experiment, a "musical note" was correctly recognized in the final step of the transformation sequence on two-thirds of the trials, but was never guessed at any of the previous steps.

These findings support the principle of structural equivalence. Apparently, subjects in these experiments could recognize emergent patterns that they did not anticipate, and in this respect they were capable of reinterpreting an image.

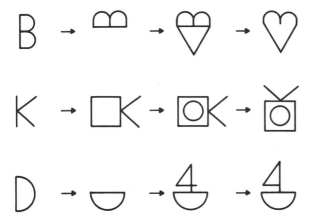

Figure 5.12
Examples of emergent patterns resulting from the imagined transformation of a starting pattern. These emergent patterns could be detected only when the subjects had
carried out the imagined transformations correctly. (from Finke, Pinker, and Farah, in
press)

5.4.4 Apparent Contradictions in Findings on Image Reinterpretation
The studies in the two previous sections lead to apparently contradictory conclusions. On the one hand, there is evidence that structurally poor parts are difficult to detect in an image, and that
perceptual reversals in classic ambiguous figures cannot be detected
in images of these figures (section 5.3). The principle of structural
equivalence cannot explain these findings. On the other hand, there
are counterexamples showing that people can detect emergent forms
in an image that would not have been deduced from initial descriptions of the objects or patterns. How does one resolve these
discrepancies?

Pinker, Farah, and I proposed (Finke, Pinker, and Farah, in press)
that classic ambiguous figures may belong to a special class. To
achieve a complete perceptual reversal of these kinds of figures
would require a global resolution of all the local ambiguities contained in the figure. For example, to perceptually reverse the Necker
cube (see again figure 5.10), the visual system has to resolve, simultaneously, local ambiguities in the concavity, depth, and orientation
of each of the corners. This may be difficult to accomplish in imagery,
especially if the parts of an image periodically fade and have to be
regenerated (as suggested by the findings of Kosslyn 1975; and Kosslyn, Reiser, Farah, and Fliegel 1983), or if the reversal process depends on low-level visual mechanisms that cannot be activated

during visualization (Finke 1980; Marr 1982; Ullman 1984; see also section 2.3.2).

Whether or not structurally inferior parts can be detected in an image probably depends on the complexity of the imagined pattern and on how completely the pattern has been segmented into meaningful, "good" parts. Structurally "poor" parts, for example, would be harder to detect if images fade as meaningful units, which would limit opportunities for mentally reorganizing or restructuring the parts (see Bower and Glass 1976; Kosslyn 1980). This may be one reason why people often fail to detect parts that are structurally "hidden" in an image, as in Reed's (1974) study, but can otherwise detect emergent forms that result from an imagined synthesis or transformation.

5.4.5 Creative Visual Synthesis in Mental Imagery

In each of the previous studies on mental synthesis, the subjects were always told exactly how to imagine combining the parts. Could people ever discover emergent patterns in the *absence* of explicit instructions for how to construct their images? If so, this would indicate that mental imagery might serve an important function in creative thinking.

There are, for instance, numerous informal accounts of mental imagery having been used in the act of making creative discoveries. One famous example is Kekule's report of having imagined a group of snakes coiled together at the very moment he discovered the molecular structure of benzene (see Shepard 1978a, 1988). There are also reports of mechanical inventions having been inspired by imagining the parts of objects combined or rearranged in original ways (Ferguson 1977). Although such accounts are intriguing, there have been few empirical studies on the extent to which people can use imagery to make creative discoveries.

Karen Slayton and I have recently conducted experiments in which subjects were given opportunities to use an unconstrained, exploratory mental synthesis to make creative discoveries under imagery laboratory conditions (Finke and Slayton 1988). We modified the general methods of the study by Finke, Pinker, and Farah (in press). At the beginning of the experiment, the subjects were shown the various kinds of parts they might be asked to use; as shown in figure 5.13, these consisted of simple geometric forms, lines, and alphanumeric characters. On each trial, the subjects closed their eyes and three of the parts were named, sometimes more than once. For example, the experimenter might call out "circle, letter T, triangle"

Figure 5.13
Parts of patterns used in experiments on creative mental synthesis. Subjects were given three of the parts at random and were instructed to imagine combining the parts to make a recognizable pattern. (from Finke and Slayton 1988)

or "square, square, number 8." The subjects were to use all three parts to try to imagine a recognizable object or pattern. They could combine or arrange the parts in any way, changing the position, orientation, or size of any part, but they could not alter the shape of a part; for example, they could not distort a circle to make it into an ellipse. It was stressed that the resulting object or pattern must be something that another person could recognize. The three parts were randomly selected in advance by a computer, so there were no intended "target" patterns on any of the trials.

After two minutes, they were told to write down the name of any object they had imagined, and then to draw the object. A group of judges then rated whether the drawings were recognizable from the names and, if so, whether the objects or patterns depicted by the drawings were notably creative. Their drawings revealed that the subjects had been able to discover a recognizable pattern on about 40 percent of the trials; of these, 15 percent were judged to be highly creative. Examples of some of these "creative" patterns are shown in figure 5.14. Although the subjects were never told to use imagery or to try to be creative, almost three-fourths of them reported, as their strategy for doing the task, that they had tried to imagine combining the parts by trial and error to mentally "see" if anything familiar "emerged." Control procedures showed that very few of the recognizable patterns and virtually none of the highly creative patterns could be predicted simply from knowing what the parts were.

These findings suggest that mental imagery can be used to explore creative combinations of parts in order to discover meaningful objects, shapes, or patterns. Thus, a mental image, like an actual physical object, can often be interpreted *after* its parts are assembled, sometimes in highly original and unexpected ways. In the Finke and

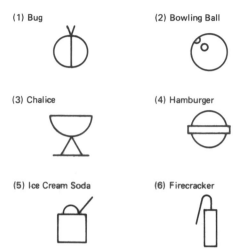

Figure 5.14
Examples of mentally synthesized patterns that were judged to be highly creative. Virtually none of these creative patterns could be predicted by the subjects or the experimenter. (from Finke and Slayton 1988)

Slayton experiments, these discoveries were unlikely to have been the result of experimenter effects or guessing strategies. Rather, they seem to have resulted from structural relationships among the parts that emerged and were detected in the imagined syntheses. This implies that the principle of structural equivalence can be extended to the domain of creative visual exploration.

5.5. Viewer-Centered vs. Object-Centered Representations

There has been much debate over whether objects are recognized using *viewer*-centered representations (how an object appears from a particular vantage point) or *object*-centered representations (in terms of the inherent, three-dimensional structure of an object). This issue, and its implications for the principle of structural equivalence, will be discussed briefly here.

5.5.1 Evidence for Viewer-Centered Representations

Experiments on mental rotation, considered in chapter 4, would suggest that memories for the shape of an object are based on how the object appears from a specific point of view. If objects were remembered solely in terms of their structural characteristics, independently of how they looked from different vantage points, mental rotation would never be necessary. Also, there are certain types of objects that are extremely difficult to recognize when presented in unfamiliar orientations. For example, irregularly shaped objects, such as wire figures, crumpled-up sheets of paper, and novel clay molds, often fail to be recognized after having been rotated in depth (Rock and DiVita 1987; Rock, DiVita, and Barbeito 1981). Such findings suggest that object recognition is based on representations that are centered on one's own viewing perspective.

5.5.2 Evidence for Object-Centered Representations

On the other hand, a memory system in which one had to remember how an object looks from every possible point of view, or which required that one always perform a mental transformation of some sort before being able to recognize the object, would be very ineffi-cient. Most familiar objects, in fact, *can* be easily recognized when seen from novel vantage points (Gibson 1969). Also, as suggested by experiments on forming memory "prototypes" (discussed in section 1.5.1), we tend to remember the average characteristics of an object, not the way it looked at any one particular time. Such findings support the existence of object-centered representations.

5.5.3 Marr's Model of Pattern Recognition

Taking into account these apparently contradictory findings, David Marr (1982) proposed a model of pattern recognition that made use of both viewer-centered and object-centered representations. Accord-ing to Marr's model, viewer-centered representations are used in the early and intermediate stages of the recognition process, where in-formation is extracted about the locations of edges and other surface features. This information is used to compute the relative depth of surfaces as seen from the viewer's perspective (which Marr calls the "2 ½ – D sketch"), and is then used to construct an object-centered representation of the three-dimensional shape of the object. The object-centered representations consist of generalized "cones," which are symmetrical components connected in a hierarchical fashion (see also Marr and Nishihara 1978; and more recently Biederman 1987). For example, a person would be recognized by having a large, gen-eralized cone in the shape of a torso, to which are connected smaller generalized cones in the shapes of arms and legs, to which are connected still smaller generalized cones in the shapes of fingers and toes. The resulting object-centered representation would allow one to recognize the person independently of how he or she was posi-tioned relative to the viewer.

One implication of Marr's model is that object-centered representations would be used to recognize an object only when the three-dimensional shape of the object could be easily extracted and distinguished from other shapes. This might explain, for example, why people rely on viewer-centered representations to compare or recognize objects whose shapes differ in terms of subtle mirror-image reflections (Corballis 1988; Shepard and Metzler 1971; see section 4.1.1), or have poorly defined or unusual internal structures (Rock and DiVita 1987). Object-centered representations, in contrast, would be used to recognize objects having well-defined and highly distinctive internal structures, or that have many moving or salient parts. There is growing evidence, in fact, that both kinds of representations can be used, depending on the nature of the object, its relation to other objects, and the demands of the experimental task (see Jolicoeur and Kosslyn 1983).

The principle of structural equivalence allows for the use of both kinds of representations in mental imagery. As shown by studies reviewed earlier in this chapter, not only can one represent the three-dimensional structure of objects in mental images (Cooper, in press; see section 5.2.2), one can also detect emergent patterns in images that are specific to particular viewing perspectives (Pinker and Finke 1980; see section 5.4.3). Moreover, some combination of viewer-centered and object-centered representations is implied by studies showing that people can imagine a three-dimensional array of objects in depth, independently of viewing perspective, while also imagining the viewer-dependent "projections" of those objects (e.g., Pinker 1980; see section 3.1.2).

5.6 Summary and Conclusions

The principle of structural equivalence states that mental images possess structural characteristics corresponding to those of actual perceived objects, such that relationships among an object's parts can be both preserved and reinterpreted. Evidence in support of this principle comes primarily from studies on mental synthesis and on emergent pattern recognitions in imagery. There are notable exceptions to the principle; for instance, mental imagery is limited when one tries to detect structurally "hidden" parts or perceptual reversals of ambiguous figures. Nevertheless, it is possible to show that people can make genuine visual discoveries in imagery, some of which are strikingly creative.

5.7 Further Explorations

5.7.1 Recommendations for Further Reading

Good introductions to the kinds of problems one encounters in developing models of pattern recognition can be found in David Marr's now-classic book *Vision* (1982) and in recent articles by Hoffman and Richards (1984), Pinker (1984), and Poggio (1984). These include difficult matters such as how objects and their parts are segmented within a visual scene, how one goes about constructing object-centered representations given viewer-centered representations, and how conceptual knowledge and expectations influence the recognition process. For a discussion of how similar kinds of problems need to be addressed in models of mental imagery, see Kosslyn (1983) and Pinker (1984). Informative reviews of earlier work on pattern recognition can be found in Lindsay and Norman (1977), Minsky and Papert (1972), Neisser (1967), and Rock (1983).

5.7.2 Creativity and the Control of Imagery

The precise connection between imagery and creativity is likely to be fairly complex. Highly creative individuals often score better on tests of ability to control images, but this relation may depend on various kinds of personality factors (Forisha 1978). One of the factors that seems to be important in using imagery creatively is the extent to which one can become "absorbed" in imagined activities, a trait related to hypnotic susceptibility (Hilgard 1970; Spanos and McPeake 1975; Tellegen and Atkinson 1974). For example, when reading a novel, highly hypnotizable individuals often imagine themselves witnessing the actions and events, in a kind of ongoing mental synthesis. Hence, it may be important both to control and to become absorbed in imagery when using imagery for creative purposes.

5.7.3 Imagery and Dreaming

The creative use of imagery is perhaps most evident in dreams. According to modern theories of dreaming, one of the functions of dreams is to "consolidate" information acquired during the waking state; that is, to integrate the information meaningfully within a conceptual framework (Cohen 1979). In this sense, dreams may allow one to achieve dramatic, emergent "recognitions" or insights (see Shepard 1978a).

In a particular kind of dream, known as a *lucid dream*, a person realizes that he or she is dreaming and is able to exert some control over what happens in the dream (Hearne 1981). In fact, one can even carry out dream "experiments," exploring the consequences of novel actions and events. For example, one can dream about floating above a room and vividly "seeing" how objects would look. There are various techniques one can use to trigger lucid dreaming, such as awakening late at night and reading part of a book before going back to sleep (see La Berge 1980). Lucid dreams may thus afford a unique opportunity for exploring the creative potential of images.

Chapter 6
Principles, Foundations, and Applications

This final chapter will consider the advantages of thinking about mental imagery in the context of general principles, recent work on the neurological foundations of imagery, and the practical implications of imagery research.

6.1 Unifying Principles vs. Formal Models

The topics considered in this book have been organized around five general principles of mental imagery. With certain exceptions, I believe that these principles have been largely confirmed by the current literature on imagery research. I have taken this approach to the study of imagery rather than attempt to formulate a formal imagery model, which would have been more in keeping with the dominant trend in cognitive psychology. In this first section I offer some reasons for why I have chosen to think about imagery in terms of general principles, beginning with a consideration of the advantages and disadvantages of formal models.

6.1.1 Advantages of Formal Models
Most theories in cognitive psychology are motivated by intuitions about the nature of mental processes. These intuitions are then developed and refined to the point where an explicit theory can be formulated and tested. Two general strategies can be distinguished for doing so: "formal focusing" and "intuitive spreading."

In the formal focusing strategy, one tries to develop formal models of the computational procedures that are likely to be carried out by information-processing mechanisms in the brain. Because there are many such computational procedures, and because the kinds of computations that are needed can vary considerably, formal models often include many different types of internal mechanisms. These mechanisms are defined by the precise manner in which they are used to process information. They are usually connected by various internal "pathways," which transfer information from one mechanism to another. Different formal models are thus distinguished by the kinds of internal mechanisms they posit and the way the mechanisms are connected. Typically, a formal model has many adjustable parameters that allow one to "fine-tune" the model, to obtain a better fit between data and theory. Hence, in using the formal focusing strategy, the process of going from intuitions to theory is largely a matter of sharpening those intuitions computationally, focusing them onto precise, quantitative theoretical frameworks.

There are obvious advantages to this approach. First, by characterizing cognitive processes in terms of the computational properties of information-processing mechanisms, one can claim to have removed some of the mystery about how the human mind works. Computational mechanisms are more tangible than intuitions. Also, because the predictions that a formal model makes are computationally more precise, they help to give the impression that cognitive psychology has the kind of solid, technical foundation that is characteristic of theories in the harder sciences (Anderson 1983; Anderson and Bower 1973).

A second advantage of constructing formal models is that they can often be tested using computer simulations. The computational power of the modern computer makes it possible to simulate even the most intricate information-processing systems. A complex theory can thus be made predictively manageable, and confirmations of the theory can be used to extend the analogy between computers and the human mind. In turn, advances in computer science can be applied to the study of cognitive processes, by using those advances to further shape and refine a formal model (Newell and Simon 1972).

A third advantage of formal models is that they can often account for a large proportion of the variance in experimental data, because they often include parameters that allow for fine adjustments in the predicted outcomes as more data is collected. These parameters can be modified without changing the overall structure of the model, and this helps to account for things like individual differences in how quickly information is processed (Sternberg 1977). Formal models can therefore have considerable explanatory power.

6.1.2 Disadvantages of Formal Models
Given these advantages, why *wouldn't* a person want to use formal models in developing a cognitive theory? One reason is that in becoming computationally more precise, a formal model is often refined to the point where it applies only to one specific kind of task. This risk increases, typically, as one tries to adjust the model to account

for more and more of the variance in performance. There are, to be sure, formal models, such as propositional models of memory (see section 1.5.5), that have avoided this problem by allowing sufficient flexibility in the way the model can be applied computationally across different kinds of tasks (e.g., Anderson 1976). Such models are usually so unconstrained, however, that they can explain virtually any finding at all by making appropriate adjustments in the structure of the model (Kosslyn 1981). Thus, whenever formal models appear to have general applicability, they may not be falsifiable.

A similar problem is that once a formal model is refined to the point where it can successfully account for the results of a particular experiment, it may have reached a theoretical dead end. If interest is then lost in the findings of that experiment, the model may simply be forgotten. On the other hand, a formal model that can be readjusted to such an extent that it could explain a wide range of findings may spread itself so thin that it becomes predictively empty. One would prefer that a theory be predictively *inspirational* when successful, leading to new research developments and conceptual advances.

6.1.3 An Example of a Computational Model of Imagery

Kosslyn and his students have developed a formal model of mental image generation that illustrates both the advantages and disadvantages of the formal focusing approach (Kosslyn 1980; Kosslyn and Shwartz 1977). This model is based on a computer analogy to how information is displayed visually on a cathode-ray tube (CRT). Image formation begins by retrieving information in long-term memory about the properties and appearances of objects. This information is stored in the form of propositions listing the features of the object and "skeletal" representations about the object's general shape. The mental image is then constructed within a spatial medium called the "visual buffer," which, like a CRT, has a limited size and resolution.

In the Kosslyn and Shwartz model, there are many distinct processes that are supposedly used for displaying images, such as FIND, PUT, REGENERATE, SCAN, ZOOM, and ROTATE. These processes serve, respectively, to locate parts on the image, to integrate a new part into an image, to keep the image from fading, to reposition the image, to adjust the size scale of the image, and to reorient the image. Each of these "components" can be built into a computer simulation to model the different ways in which imagery might be used. Moreover, these components can function independently, resulting in a "modular" imagery system (see Fodor 1983).

The complete working model is comprehensive and provides a computational explanation for many of the findings on imagery that have been discussed in this book (e.g., see Kosslyn 1980, 1981, 1983). The model also helps to demystify the nature of imagery by relating the generation of a mental image to the more explicit and readily quantifiable procedures used in generating visual displays on a computer (Kosslyn, Pinker, Smith, and Shwartz 1979). Another virtue of the Kosslyn and Shwartz model is that it emphasizes that imagery is not a single, unitary skill. For example, Kosslyn, Brunn, Cave, and Wallach (1984) have found that people vary in their ability to carry out different types of imagery tasks, and that at least some of these differences can be accounted for in terms of the various components proposed in the model. Thus, the model can potentially account for much of the variance in how imagery tasks are performed.

The main difficulty with this model, as with other models based on computer analogies of cognitive processes, is that it gains explanatory power at the expense of predictive power. To a large extent, the precise way in which the many components are coordinated in the Kosslyn and Shwartz model depends arbitrarily on the results of imagery experiments. Had those results turned out differently, the model might also have "accounted" for them. Consequently, although the model is capable of generating some new predictions (see Kosslyn 1980, 1981, 1987), they are largely predictions of *refinement*, and their theoretical interest is limited by the extent of one's ongoing commitment to the model.

6.1.4 *Advantages of Searching for General, Unifying Principles*
An alternative approach, which is the one adopted in this book, is based on the strategy of allowing intuitions to spread without artificially restricting them. In so doing, one hopes to discover broad principles that unify knowledge within a relatively large research domain. By allowing intuitions to spread freely, one is more likely to discover the underlying connections relating a wide range of findings. These intuitions can then develop naturally into predictively powerful unifying principles.

This "intuitive spreading" strategy is, in many respects, just the opposite of the formal focusing strategy. Instead of trying to demystify cognitive processes, one tries to acquire a broad, enlightened understanding of their general nature and purpose. Instead of trying to account for all of the variance in a specific cognitive task, one tries to identify the general characteristics of a cognitive process that are common to many tasks. Instead of trying to simulate cognitive processes, one tries to stimulate new discoveries.

With this approach, the disadvantages of using computational models to motivate imagery research are largely avoided. Whereas formal models tend to be complicated and are often limited in their applicability, unifying principles, such as those that have been considered in this book, are relatively simple and apply over broad domains. There is thus little danger of a unifying principle becoming overspecialized. Also, unifying principles are much less likely to reach theoretical dead ends. The development of a unifying principle is more of a "reaching out" process than a "focusing in on" process; as such, there is room for theoretical growth. This is the reason, in fact, why unifying principles often inspire entirely new lines of research.

For example, the principle of implicit encoding has motivated new findings on techniques for improving one's memory (section 1.5). The principle of perceptual equivalence has motivated research on whether perceptual aftereffects can be created using imagery (section 2.3). The principle of spatial equivalence has led to new understandings about the nature of cognitive maps (section 3.4). The principle of transformational equivalence has inspired research on the inertial properties of mental transformations (section 4.5). And the principle of structural equivalence has led to new work on the reinterpretation of images (section 5.4). I doubt that formal models of imagery would have motivated such a diverse variety of new studies.

Kosslyn (1983), among others, has argued that complex models of the mind are needed because the mind itself is so complex. But this is not necessarily true. What seems complex at first can often become simple and understandable once the underlying principles are discovered. This has usually been the case in other fields of science; the laws of physics, for example, are surprisingly simple, given nature's complexities (Feynman 1967). On the contrary, by accepting complexity as theoretically unavoidable, one runs the risk of *not* discovering the fundamental, unifying principles.

Geoffrey Loftus (1985), for instance, has raised the provocative question of whether computer simulations are seducing us away from doing real creative thinking in the behavioral sciences. He offers the hypothetical example of whether Kepler's laws of planetary motion ever would have been discovered had Kepler had access to the modern computer. This would have enabled him to construct simulation models of the planetary orbits using Ptolemy's complex system of epicycles, for he would then have had the computational power to do so. But because Kepler was both unwilling and unable to develop such a model, he was, fortunately, motivated to find simple, underlying principles. Loftus makes a similar argument for why modern computer simulations might inhibit us from seeking to find simplicity in psychological laws.

6.1.5 Criticisms of the Search for Unifying Principles

Pinker and Kosslyn (1983) have criticized a theoretical reliance on general principles in conducting imagery research, on the grounds that such principles usually fail to specify the details of the underlying cognitive mechanisms. The principle of transformational equivalence, for example, says nothing about the nature of the computational processes that are engaged during an imagined transformation. In this respect, a unifying principle may not provide a satisfying explanation of how a cognitive process works. On the other hand, formal models that purport to explain data by specifying the details of cognitive mechanisms and their numerous interconnections may be equally unsatisfying. They have much explanatory power but may yield few basic understandings, and in this sense may be conceptually inhibiting.

A second criticism of developing imagery theories around unifying principles is that one can always find exceptions to the principles. For example, the principle of structural equivalence does not hold for certain kinds of reversible figures (section 5.3). Similarly, the principle of perceptual equivalence does not apply to perceptual processes occurring at the most peripheral levels of the visual system (section 2.3). However, a unifying principle is not necessarily *disconfirmed* by these kinds of exceptions, if what they do is merely restrict the domain of the principle's applicability. In physics, for example, there are exceptions to Newton's laws of motion that restrict its range of validity to nonrelativistic situations. One would not, however, want to abandon Newton's laws because of these exceptions. If a principle must be severely restricted, or if it doesn't result in a convergence of findings, then it should be abandoned, but I do not think this is true of any of the principles that have been proposed in this book.

6.1.6 Ecological Considerations in Mental Representation

Another reason why one might wish to think about cognitive processes in terms of unifying principles is that these principles are often *ecologically* significant (see Gibson 1979; Neisser 1976). For example, Shepard (1984, 1987) has proposed that many of the laws governing the physical properties of natural objects and their motions have been internalized into the mental structures of living organisms. This would afford a tremendous ecological advantage when interacting with the physical world. Unifying principles that tie together basic findings about cognitive processes are therefore likely to reflect these same ecological constraints. Such constraints might be overlooked, however, if one's intuitions were artificially constrained by the strictly computational considerations of formal models.

6.2 Neurological Foundations of Mental Imagery

Ultimately, many of the debates surrounding the nature of imagery will be decided by neurological studies (Anderson 1978). In particular, if one could show that mental imagery makes use of certain regions of the brain that have specialized functions, one could narrow down the range of possible explanations for the findings of imagery experiments (Farah 1988; Finke 1980; Kosslyn 1987).

6.2.1 Evidence for Left Hemisphere Involvement in Mental Image Generation

Most people assume that imagery is a "right hemisphere" skill, largely because of its popular association with "global" processing and creativity (e.g., Springer and Deutsch 1981). However, recent neurological studies suggest that this widespread belief is almost certainly wrong. Although the recognition of visual shapes and spatial relations may, to some extent, be localized in the right cerebral hemisphere, there is little evidence supporting the claim that mental imagery is localized there as well (Erlichman and Barrett 1983). On the contrary, the process of generating a mental image appears to be a *left* hemisphere function.

Martha Farah (1984) has reviewed a large number of studies investigating the loss of mental imagery following brain damage. She found a consistent pattern in these studies: patients who had difficulty generating images tended to have damage to the posterior region of their left cerebral hemisphere. This deficit in image generation could be distinguished from other aspects of visual information processing by analyzing the kinds of tasks that the patients could perform. For example, a patient might be able to recognize and draw visually presented objects, but be unable to draw or describe the objects from memory, suggesting that the problem lies in generating images of objects.

Farah et al. (unpublished) have attempted to localize more precisely the regions in the left cerebral hemisphere that are involved in mental image generation. Using electrophysiological recording techniques, they found that neural activity in both the occipital and posterior temporal areas of the left cerebral hemisphere increased when subjects were instructed to visualize objects denoted by visually presented words. Experimental controls showed that this change in cortical activity was not due to the visual effort required to read the words; instead, it was specific to the act of generating the images.

As Farah et al. concluded, these findings cannot easily be explained in terms of propositions or other nonvisual forms of internal representation, because the occipital lobe of the cerebral cortex is known to process information that is predominantly visual. Thus, it is apparent that the imagery used in this task was *visual* imagery, as opposed to some amodal or purely spatial form of imagery (see section 1.5.4). Similarly, tacit knowledge, experimenter bias, or other artifacts stemming from demand characteristics can be ruled out, because it is very unlikely that a subject would know, tacitly or otherwise, which areas of the brain are supposed to be activated when recalling how an object looks. For that matter, even if subjects did possess this knowledge, it is unclear how they would voluntarily simulate a characteristic pattern of brain activity in those particular regions.

6.2.2 Studies on Split-Brain Patients

Further evidence that mental image generation occurs in the left cerebral hemisphere has come from studies on split-brain patients. These are patients who, for various medical reasons, have had their corpus callosum severed, which is the large neural pathway that connects the cerebral hemispheres. Such patients often show striking dissociations in verbal and spatial functions when stimuli are presented to either hemisphere alone (e.g., Gazzaniga 1970).

Kosslyn, Holtzman, Farah, and Gazzaniga (1985) conducted an extensive investigation of the imagery skills of one such patient. Their experiments revealed that the right hemisphere clearly shows an imagery deficiency relative to the left hemisphere. For example, in one experiment the subject was presented with a lower-case letter to either hemisphere, and his task was to say whether or not the upper-case version of the letter contained any curved lines. This task was therefore designed to elicit, from memory, detailed mental images of the letters. The subject's left hemisphere was accurate on all of the trials, whereas his right hemisphere was accurate on only 70 percent of the trials. In contrast, there were no differences between the hemispheres on variations of the task in which the upper-case letters were actually presented, were retained briefly in short-term memory, or were drawn by the subject. This pattern of results suggests that the right hemisphere is deficient in generating mental images.

Kosslyn et al. went on to perform other experiments to try to determine whether the problem had to do with generating images in general, or only those images that contained detailed visual features. The subject was given the names of pairs of animals that were similar in size, and had to say which of the two were larger. This kind of task typically yields the symbolic distance effect, which, as discussed in section 1.5.2, need not depend on using imagery that is specifically visual. In this case, both hemispheres performed equally well. Kosslyn et al. then conducted a slightly different version of this task, presenting single animal names to the subject and asking him to indicate whether the animal's ears protruded above the top of its head or pointed down. This time, the right hemisphere was only half as accurate as the left hemisphere. This suggested that although both hemispheres can be used to generate "sketchy" or amodal images, the left hemisphere is superior in generating images that contain accurate visual details. Kosslyn (1987) has interpreted these findings as supporting his componential model of imagery; in particular, that the PUT operation is executed specifically by the left hemisphere.

Laterality differences have also been studied using normal subjects, where the measure of interest is the time it takes to perform an imagery task using the right and left hemispheres. These studies, too, have shown a left hemisphere superiority for generating images that contain many visual details (Farah 1986; see also Kosslyn 1987).

6.2.3 Dissociations of Identification and Localization in Imagery

Over the past twenty years, much evidence has accumulated suggesting that the visual identification of objects can be dissociated from visually guided orientation and localization (Held 1970; Sagi and Julesz 1985; Schneider 1969; Teuber 1978). For example, patients who suffer from visual *agnosia* have trouble identifying objects but can easily locate them, whereas patients who have trouble orienting themselves to objects can often identify them quite easily. In other words, people can sometimes identify *what* something is without knowing *where* it is, and vice versa.

Evidence that a similar kind of dissociation exists in mental imagery was reported recently by Levine, Warach, and Farah (1985). They studied two patients who suffered deficiencies in both imagery and perception. The first patient, who had had a right anterior temporal lobotomy, had considerable difficulty describing faces of familiar people or the appearances of animals from memory, although he showed no impairment in spatial imagery and was able to give precise directions for how to get to various landmarks in his city. The second patient, who had had bilateral lesions of the parieto-occipital regions of his cortex, could easily describe the appearances of faces and objects from memory, but could not give simple directions for how to get to familiar places. These imagery deficiencies were reflected in corresponding perceptual deficiencies; the first patient had trouble recognizing familiar objects, whereas the second patient had trouble identifying spatial relationships among objects. Similarly, Farah et al. (in press) have reported a brain-damaged patient who has normal spatial imagery but cannot perform any of the standard tests used to measure visual imagery. These findings further establish the distinction between visual and spatial imagery (see chapters 2 and 3). Also, they reinforce the conclusions of previous studies—for example, those considered in chapter 2—that at least some neural mechanisms in the visual system are common to imagery and perception.

6.3 Practical Applications of Mental Imagery

In addition to some of the applications mentioned in previous chapters (e.g., using imagery to retrieve information from memory, to influence perceptual processes, to judge spatial relations, to identify misoriented objects, and to discover emergent structures), imagery has a number of other practical applications. These will be considered presently.

6.3.1 Reasoning and Problem Solving

There are many types of problems for which imagery can provide short cuts to the final solution. One example comes from studies on verifying ordered syllogisms. For instance, when given that "Tom is taller than Sam" and "John is shorter than Sam," and asked to say which of the three is the tallest, people can determine the answer by imagining spatial arrays in which the individuals are ordered along the dimension of size (Huttenlocher 1968). A similar technique can be used for other dimensions of comparison, such as intelligence or friendliness (e.g., "Mary is friendlier than Susan, but Jane is not as friendly as Mary"; "Who is the friendliest of the three?"). The spatial characteristics of mental images can therefore represent physical or conceptual relationships among people, places, or things, allowing one to make decisions about those relationships without having to carry out an extensive logical analysis (see also Beveridge and Parkins 1987).

Imagery can also contribute to efficient problem solving by mentally simulating physical events. One such example is the "monk" problem, proposed by the Gestalt psychologists and considered more recently by McKim (1980) and Kosslyn (1983). A monk decides to walk up a mountain one morning to meditate at its summit. He arrives late in the afternoon, after stopping to rest along the way, and spends the night meditating. The next morning he walks back down the mountain, along the same path, and returns early in the afternoon. Was the monk ever at the same point on the path at the same time of day on each of the two days?

The solution is easy using a mental simulation of the monk's walk. Imagine duplicate monks, one starting up the mountain, and the other coming down. If they both left in the morning, and traveled along the same path, they would surely pass each other at some point, regardless of how quickly they walked or where they stopped to rest. Therefore, there must exist a point where the monk would be at the same time of day on each day.

Mental simulations can also enable the problem solver to consider extreme situations. An example is given by Levine (1987). Two flag-poles, each 100 feet tall, are connected at the top by a piece of rope 150 feet long. The rope is 25 feet off the ground at its lowest point. How far apart are the flagpoles?

One doesn't need calculus to solve this problem. Start by imagining the flagpoles with the connecting rope sagging down. Try imagining the flagpoles as far apart as possible—which is 150 feet, the length of the rope. The rope is now 100 feet off the ground, neglecting the effects of its own weight. Clearly, this is not the right solution, since the rope is supposed to be 25 feet off the ground. Now imagine moving the flagpoles as close together as possible. How far above the ground is the rope now hanging?

Mental simulations can thus provide insights that might have been overlooked if one only considered formal or analytical methods in solving problems. For example, one might gain new insights into how to solve problems in physics or mechanics by imagining the way objects would move or interact with one another (Hayes 1973; Simon and Barenfeld 1969). In addition, imagined simulations could be combined with other problem-solving techniques, such as the use of analogies or the technique of working backward, to help one arrive at correct solutions (see Polya 1957; Wickelgren 1974).

Even in such everyday tasks as contemplating how to arrange furniture in a room, or books on a bookshelf, imagined simulations could provide useful insights and save considerable effort in wasted trial and error. Note that the principles of spatial and transformational equivalence make such applications possible. If these principles were not valid, that is, if imagery could not faithfully depict spatial ar-rangements of objects and their transformations, then imagery would be of little value as a problem-solving aid.

6.3.2 Therapeutic Insights Using Imagery

There are many clinical uses of mental imagery (see reviews in Sheehan 1972; Sheikh 1983); only a few of these will be mentioned here. One is to use imagery, often in conjunction with hypnosis, to retrieve lost memories. As discussed in section 1.5.2, however, this use of imagery is now controversial, because memories elicited in this way are subject to various kinds of distortions, including fabrication. Whether such methods are effective would depend on whether or not the principle of implicit encoding applies (see section 1.4).

Another clinical application of imagery is in desensitizing people to anxiety-producing objects or situations (Singer 1974; Wolpe 1969). For example, in the treatment of phobias a helpful technique, *systematic desensitization*, is to have a person visualize the feared object in conjunction with relaxation training, until the object no longer elicits an anxiety reaction. The advantage of using imagery is that one can mentally "approach" the feared object in progressive stages, without actually having the object present. Such methods would be effective to the extent that the principle of perceptual equivalence applies, since imagined experiences are used in place of actual perceptual experiences.

Further clinical applications of imagery might stem from people's ability to make creative discoveries in their images. As discussed in section 5.4.5, recent studies have demonstrated that such discoveries can often be made following an imagined synthesis or transformation. Modern Gestalt therapists, for example, could make use of visualization for precisely this purpose, in attempting to get clients to discover solutions to problems in their lives (e.g., Perls 1970). For instance, a person might be encouraged to imagine having a fight with a friend, to mentally "discover" things about their relationship, not previously realized, that were causing certain difficulties. The principle of structural equivalence would bear crucially on the success of these applications.

6.3.3 Benefits of Mental Practice

Professional athletes have often claimed to use what has been called "mental practice" in preparing themselves for a sporting event. For example, the golfer Jack Nicklaus (1974) reports that he imagines hitting the golf ball and mentally "seeing" where it goes, before actually hitting it. Tennis players, basketball players, and gymnasts have likewise made similar claims about the benefits of mental practice (Richardson 1967, 1969; Suinn 1980). In preparing yourself to face an opponent in a tennis match, for instance, you might discover the best strategy to use by imagining hitting the ball to certain places on the court and then imagining how well the opponent could return it.

These techniques work, I think, for two reasons. First, there is something called the "ideomotor" effect, which refers to a subtle tendency for movements to be initiated automatically whenever the movements are imagined (Greenwald 1970; Hilgard 1965, 1977). This tendency would allow a person to "prime" the appropriate movements in advance. Second, these methods could enable one to mentally *coordinate* a sequence of movements. For instance, one could try to coordinate the hand and foot movements involved in serving a tennis ball by repeatedly imagining carrying out those movements and mentally correcting any errors. (See also experiments on using imagery to induce changes in visual-motor coordination, discussed in section 2.3.5.)

The benefits of such methods would depend, though, on how familiar a person is with the actual consequences of the imagined movements. For example, I doubt if a beginning basketball player could learn to shoot free throws accurately just by imagining doing so, without having prior experience at the task. In fact, one might even *inhibit* the eventual learning of a skill by imagining the wrong consequences of actions. On the other hand, if someone were already skilled in making one kind of basketball shot, it might be possible to shorten the time it would take to master a different shot by using mental practice. The principles of perceptual and transformational equivalence are both relevant to the potential success of these techniques.

6.3.4 Imagery and Perceptual Learning
Gibson (1966, 1979) has proposed that perceptual learning occurs whenever one repeatedly perceives the same object, pattern, or event over time. This is why, for example, one can learn to see things in a painting that were not apparent when the painting was initially inspected. Can perceptual learning also be achieved in imagery?

This book has reviewed a number of studies showing that people can mentally synthesize the parts of objects (section 5.1), can detect emergent forms in imagery (section 5.4), and can use imagery to facilitate perceptual discriminations (section 2.4). It should therefore be possible to achieve some degree of perceptual learning, in Gibson's sense, by repeatedly imagining that one is inspecting an object, even if the object has never previously been seen. For example, if you were shown the mythical animal that was described at the beginning of the previous chapter, consisting of the body of a lion and the legs of an ostrich, you could probably recognize the animal quite easily had you clearly imagined it. Future studies on imagery are needed to explore this possibility. As in the case of mental practice, the success of using imagery in perceptual learning would probably depend on how accurately one imagined the objects or events (see also section 5.7.2).

6.3.5 Implications for the Visual Arts

The role that imagery plays in the development and appreciation of art has been well documented, particularly in the classic works of Rudolf Arnheim (1954, 1969). Arnheim showed, for instance, how many of the interesting effects created by an artist—for example, the effects of balance and depth in a painting—could be understood from the premise that much of our thinking is visual rather than analytical. Indeed, it is often claimed that one of the purposes of art is to create meaningful images in the mind of the perceiver (Lindauer 1977).

If perceptual learning can occur in imagery, it may also be possible to "create" a work of art entirely within one's imagination. If so, imagery might be able to take over the functions of perception completely, enabling an artist to continue working even if the crucial sense is impaired. Beethoven's ability to compose music after becoming deaf is perhaps the most famous example. There are also cases where a person continued to paint after becoming totally blind by relying on visual imagery (Finke 1986a). The principles of perceptual and structural equivalence would govern the extent to which imagery could be used to guide artistic creation in such cases (see again section 5.4.5).

6.3.6 Further Practical Implications

The principles of mental imagery also extend to many other professions. Doctors, for example, must frequently visualize the relative positions of internal organs and other bodily parts. An architect might invent a new design for a building by imagining a novel arrangement of shapes and forms. Lawyers may have to determine whether an eyewitness's testimony is based on real or imagined experiences. Archeologists often have to mentally reconstruct ancient structures out of existing pieces. Good writers can create vivid images in the minds of readers, using the right words and descriptions. In fact, it's hard to think of any profession in which the skilled use of imagery would not be of some value.

6.4 Concluding Remarks

I have proposed that there are five imagery principles that provide, at the present time, a fairly complete description of the major characteristics of mental imagery. No doubt these principles may have to be further qualified as additional imagery studies are conducted, just as laws in the physical sciences often need to be qualified as new discoveries are made. But as I have argued, this would not necessarily invalidate the principles. It is also possible, of course, that *deeper* principles will eventually emerge, tying together the present imagery principles in more fundamental ways. For example, Shepard's principle of the second-order isomorphism, discussed in section 3.5.1, encompasses aspects of both the principle of spatial equivalence and the principle of transformational equivalence. The emergence of deeper principles over time is also characteristic of how principles evolve in the physical sciences.

In bringing together findings in support of these principles, I have made an effort to consider alternative explanations for the findings, such as verbal processes, propositions, tacit knowledge, experimenter bias, task demands, and eye movements. Although each of these accounts could explain certain of these findings in isolation, I do not believe that any of them can provide a satisfactory explanation when the findings are considered as a whole. Rather, I believe that the overall covergence of evidence provided by these findings confirms the general proposal that mental images have demonstrable, functional properties.

References

Anderson, J. R. (1976). *Language, memory, and thought*. Hillsdale, N. J.: Erlbaum.

Anderson, J. R. (1978). Arguments concerning representations for mental imagery. *Psychological Review* 85:249–277.

Anderson, J. R. (1983). *The architecture of cognition*. Cambridge, Mass.: Harvard University Press.

Anderson, J. R., and Bower, G. H. (1973). *Human associative memory*. New York: Wiley.

Anderson, R. E. (1982). Speech imagery is not always faster than visual imagery. *Memory & Cognition* 10:371–380.

Anderson, R. E. (1984). Did I do it or did I only imagine doing it? *Journal of Experimental Psychology: General* 113:594–613.

Anstis, S. M., and Moulden, B. P. (1970). After effect of seen movement: Evidence for peripheral and central components. *Quarterly Journal of Experimental Psychology* 22:222–229.

Appelle, S. (1972). Perception and discrimination as a function of stimulus orientation: The "oblique effect" in man and animals. *Psychological Bulletin* 89:266–273.

Arnheim, R. (1954). *Art and visual perception*. Berkeley: University of California Press.

Arnheim, R. (1969). *Visual thinking*. Berkeley: University of California Press.

Attneave, F. (1971). Multistability in perception. *Scientific American* 225:62–71.

Attneave, F., and Arnoult, M. D. (1956). The quantitative study of shape and pattern perception. *Psychological Bulletin* 53:221–227.

Attneave, F., and Farrar, P. (1977). The visual world behind the head. *American Journal of Psychology* 90:549–563.

Attneave, F., and Pierce, C. R. (1978). Accuracy of extrapolating a pointer into perceived and imagined space. *American Journal of Psychology* 91:371–387.

Aulhorn, R., and Harms, H. (1972). Visual perimetry. In D. Jameson and L. M. Hurvich, ed., *Handbook of sensory physiology: Visual psychophysics*. New York: Springer-Verlag.

Babcock, M. K., and Freyd, J. J. (in press). The perception of dynamic information in static handwritten forms. *American Journal of Psychology*.

Baird, J. C. (1970). *Psychophysical analysis of visual space*. Oxford: Pergamon Press.

Baird, J. C. (1979). Studies of the cognitive representation of spatial relations. *Journal of Experimental Psychology: General* 108:90–106.

Baird, J. C., Wagner, M., and Noma, E. (1982). Impossible cognitive spaces. *Geographic Analysis* 14:204–216.

Banks, W. P. (1981). Assessing relations between imagery and perception. *Journal of Experimental Psychology: Human Perception and Performance* 7:844–847.

Bannon, L. (1981). An investigation of image scanning. Doctoral dissertation, University of Western Ontario, London, Canada.

Barber, T. X. (1964). Hypnotically hallucinated colors and their negative afterimages. *American Journal of Psychology* 77:313–318.

Bartlett, F. C. (1932). *Remembering*. Cambridge: Cambridge University Press.

Bassman, E. S. (1978). Cognitive processes in imagined and perceived cube-folding. Doctoral dissertation, Stanford University.

Beech, J. R., and Allport, D. A. (1978). Visualization of compound scenes. *Perception* 7:129–138.

Beller, H. K. (1971). Priming: Effects of advance information on matching. *Journal of Experimental Psychology* 87:176–182.

Besner, D., and Coltheart, M. (1976). Mental size scaling examined. *Memory & Cognition* 4:525–531.

Bethell-Fox, C. E., and Shepard, R. N. (1988). Mental rotation: Effects of stimulus complexity and familiarity. *Journal of Experimental Psychology: Human Perception and Performance* 14:12–23.

Betts, G. H. (1909). *The distribution and functions of mental imagery*. New York: Columbia University Press.

Beveridge, M., and Parkins, E. (1987). Visual representation in analogue problem solving. *Memory & Cognition* 15:230–237.

Biederman, I. (1987). Recognition-by-components: A theory of human image understanding. *Psychological Review* 94:115–147.

Block, N. (1981). *Imagery*. Cambridge, Mass.: M.I.T. Press.

Boring, E. G. (1950). *A history of experimental psychology*. Englewood Cliffs, N.J.: Prentice-Hall.

Bower, G. H. (1970). Imagery as a relational organizer in associative learning. *Journal of Verbal Learning and Verbal Behavior* 9:529–533.

Bower, G. H. (1972). Mental imagery and associative learning. In L. W. Gregg, ed., *Cognition in learning and memory*. New York: Wiley.

Bower, G. H., and Glass, A. L. (1976). Structural units and the redintegrative power of picture fragments. *Journal of Experimental Psychology: Human Learning and Memory* 2:456–466.

Broerse, J., and Crassini, B. (1980). The influence of imagery ability on color aftereffects produced by physically present and imagined induction stimuli. *Perception & Psychophysics* 28:560–568.

Broerse, J., and Crassini, B. (1984). Investigations of perception and imagery using CAEs: The role of experimental design and psychophysical method. *Perception & Psychophysics* 35:155–164.

Brooks, L. R. (1967). The suppression of visualization by reading. *Quarterly Journal of Experimental Psychology* 19:289–299.

Brooks, L. R. (1968). Spatial and verbal components of the act of recall. *Canadian Journal of Psychology* 22:349–368.

Brooks, L. R. (1970). An extension of the conflict between visualization and reading. *Quarterly Journal of Experimental Psychology* 22:91–96.

Bugelski, B. R. (1970). Words and things and images. *American Psychologist* 25:1002–1012.

Bundesen, C., and Larsen, A. (1975). Visual transformation of size. *Journal of Experimental Psychology: Human Perception and Performance* 1:214–220.

Bundesen, C., Larsen, A., and Farrell, J. E. (1981). Mental transformations of size and orientation. In A. D. Baddeley and J. B. Long, eds., *Attention and performance*, vol. 9. Hillsdale, N. J.: Erlbaum.

Campbell, F. W., Kulikowski, J. J., and Levinson, J. (1966). The effect of orientation on the visual resolution of gratings. *Journal of Physiology* (London) 187:427–436.

Campbell, F. W., and Robson, J. G. (1968). Application of Fourier analysis to the visibility of gratings. *Journal of Physiology* (London) 197:551–556.

Carmichael, L., Hogan, H. P., and Walter, A. A. (1932). An experimental study of the effect of language on the reproduction of visually perceived form. *Journal of Experimental Psychology* 15:73–86.

Carpenter, P. A., and Eisenberg, P. (1978). Mental rotation and the frame of reference in blind and sighted individuals. *Perception & Psychophysics* 23:117–124.

Cavanaugh, P., and Favreau, O. E. (1980). Motion aftereffect: A global mechanism for the perception of rotation. *Perception* 9:175–182.

Chambers, D., and Reisberg, D. (1985). Can mental images be ambiguous? *Journal of Experimental Psychology: Human Perception and Performance* 11:317–328.

Chase, W. G., and Simon, H. A. (1973). Perception in chess. *Cognitive Psychology* 4:55–81.

Clark, H. H., and Chase, W. G. (1972). On the process of comparing sentences against pictures. *Cognitive Psychology* 3:472–517.

Cohen, D. B. (1979). *Sleep and dreaming: Origins, nature and functions.* New York: Pergamon.

Cohen, M. M. (1967). Continuous versus terminal visual feedback in prism aftereffects. *Perceptual and Motor Skills* 24:1295–1302.

Conrad, R. (1964). Acoustic confusion in immediate memory. *British Journal of Psychology* 55:75–84.

Cooper, L. A. (1975). Mental rotation of random two-dimensional shapes. *Cognitive Psychology* 7:20–43.

Cooper, L. A. (1976a). Demonstration of a mental analog of an external rotation. *Perception & Psychophysics* 19:296–302.

Cooper, L. A. (1976b). Individual differences in visual comparison processes. *Perception & Psychophysics* 19:433–444.

Cooper, L. A. (in press). Mental models of the structure of visual objects. In B. Shepp and S. Ballesteros, eds., *Object perception: Structure and process.* Hillsdale, N. J.: Erlbaum.

Cooper, L. A., and Podgorny, P. (1976). Mental transformations and visual comparison processes: Effects of complexity and similarity. *Journal of Experimental Psychology: Human Perception and Performance* 2:503–514.

Cooper, L. A., and Regan, D. T. (1982). Attention, perception, and intelligence. In R. Sternberg, ed., *Handbook of human intelligence.* Cambridge: Cambridge University Press.

Cooper, L. A., and Shepard, R. N. (1973a). Chronometric studies of the rotation of mental images. In W. G. Chase, ed., *Visual information processing.* New York: Academic Press.

Cooper, L. A., and Shepard, R. N. (1973b). The time required to prepare for a rotated stimulus. *Memory & Cognition* 1:246–250.

Cooper, L. A., and Shepard, R. N. (1975). Mental transformations in the identification of left and right hands. *Journal of Experimental Psychology: Human Perception and Performance* 1:48–56.

Cooper, L. A., and Shepard, R. N. (1978). Transformations on representations of objects in space. In E. C. Carterette and M. P. Friedman, eds., *Handbook of perception,* vol. 8. New York: Academic Press.

Cooper, L. A., and Shepard, R. N. (1984). Turning something over in the mind. *Scientific American* 251:106–114.

Corballis, M. C. (1986). Is mental rotation controlled or automatic? *Memory & Cognition* 14:124–128.

Corballis, M. C. (1988). Recognition of disoriented shapes. *Psychological Review* 95:115–123.

Corballis, M. C., and Roldan, C. E. (1975). Detection of symmetry as a function of angular orientation. *Journal of Experimental Psychology: Human Perception and Performance* 1:221–230.

Coren, S., and Girgus, J. S. (1978). *Seeing is deceiving: The psychology of visual illusions.* Hillsdale, N. J.: Erlbaum.

Craik, F. I. M., and Lockhart, R. S. (1972). Levels of processing: A framework for memory research. *Journal of Verbal Learning and Verbal Behavior* 11:671–684.

Craik, F. I. M., and Tulving, E. (1975). Depth of processing and the retention of words in episodic memory. *Journal of Experimental Psychology: General* 104:268–294.

Dennett, D. C. (1978). *Brainstorms.* Montgomery, Vt.: Bradford Books.

Di Vesta, F. J., Ingersoll, G., and Sunshine, P. A. (1971). A factor analysis of imagery tests. *Journal of Verbal Learning and Verbal Behavior* 10:471–479.

Dixon, P., and Just, M. A. (1978). Normalization of irrelevant dimensions in stimulus comparisons. *Journal of Experimental Psychology: Human Perception and Performance* 4:36–46.

Downs, R. M., and Stea, D. (1977). *Maps in minds: Reflections on cognitive mapping.* New York: Harper & Row.

Erdelyi, M. H. (1974). A new look at the new look: Perceptual defense and vigilance. *Psychology Review* 81:1–25.

Erdelyi, M. H., and Becker, J. (1974). Hypermnesia for pictures: Incremental memory for pictures but not words in multiple recall trials. *Cognitive Psychology* 6:159–171.

Erickson, M. H., and Erickson, E. M. (1938). The hypnotic induction of hallucinatory color vision followed by pseudo-negative after-images. *Journal of Experimental Psychology* 22:581–588.

Erlichman, H., and Barrett, J. (1983). Right hemisphere specialization for mental imagery: A review of the evidence. *Brain and Cognition* 2:55–76.

Evans, G. W. (1980). Environmental cognition. *Psychological Bulletin* 88:259–287.

Farah, M. J. (1984). The neurological basis of mental imagery: A componential analysis. *Cognition* 18:245–272.

Farah, M. J. (1985). Psychophysical evidence for a shared representational medium for mental images and percepts. *Journal of Experimental Psychology: General* 114:91–103.

Farah, M. J. (1986). The laterality of mental image generation: A test with normal subjects. *Neuropsychologica* 24:541–551.

Farah, M. J. (1988). Is visual imagery really visual? Overlooked evidence from neuropsychology. *Psychological Review* 95:307–317.

Farah, M. J. (in press). Mechanisms of imagery-perception interactions. *Journal of Experimental Psychology: Human Perception and Performance.*

Farah, M. J., Hammond, K. M., Levine, D. N., and Calvanio, R. (in press). Visual and spatial mental imagery: Dissociable systems of representation. *Cognitive Psychology.*

Farah, M. J., and Kosslyn, S. M. (1981). Structure and strategy in image generation. *Cognitive Science* 4:371–383.

Farah, M. J., Peronnet, F., Weisberg, L. L., and Perrin, F. (unpublished). Brain activity underlying mental imagery: Event-related potentials during mental image generation.

Farah, M. J., and Smith, A. F. (1983). Perceptual interference and facilitation with auditory imagery. *Perception & Psychophysics* 33:475–478.

Farrell, J. E., and Shepard, R. N. (1981). Shape, orientation, and apparent rotational motion. *Journal of Experimental Psychology: Human Perception and Performance* 7:477–486.

Ferguson, E. S. (1977). The mind's eye: Nonverbal thought in technology. *Science* 197:827–836.

Feynman, R. (1967). *The character of physical law.* Cambridge, Mass.: M.I.T. Press.

Finke, R. A. (1979a). The functional equivalence of mental images and errors of movement. *Cognitive Psychology* 11:235–264.

Finke, R. A. (1979b). Experimental investigations of imagery reafference. Doctoral dissertation, Massachusetts Institute of Technology, 1979. *Dissertation Abstracts International, 10,* 3994B (University Microfilms No. 79-24841).

Finke, R. A. (1980). Levels of equivalence in imagery and perception. *Psychological Review* 87:113–132.

Finke, R. A. (1981). Interpretations of imagery-induced McCollough effects. *Perception & Psychophysics* 30:94–95.

Finke, R. A. (1985). Theories relating mental imagery to perception. *Psychological Bulletin* 98:236–259.

Finke, R. A. (1986a). Mental imagery and the visual system. *Scientific American* 254:88–95.

Finke, R. A. (1986b). Some consequences of visualization in pattern identification and detection. *American Journal of Psychology* 99:257–274.

Finke, R. A. (unpublished). Feature interactions in imagery and perception.

Finke, R. A., and Freyd, J. J. (1985). Transformations of visual memory induced by implied motions of pattern elements. *Journal of Experimental Psychology: Learning, Memory, and Cognition* 11:780–794.

Finke, R. A., Freyd, J. J., and Shyi, G. C.-W. (1986). Implied velocity and acceleration induce transformations of visual memory. *Journal of Experimental Psychology: General* 115:175–188.

Finke, R. A., Johnson, M. J., and Shyi, G. C.-W. (1988). Memory confusions for real and imagined completions of symmetrical visual patterns. *Memory & Cognition* 16:133–137.

Finke, R. A., and Kosslyn, S. M. (1980). Mental imagery acuity in the peripheral visual field. *Journal of Experimental Psychology: Human Perception and Performance* 6:244–264.

Finke, R. A., and Kurtzman, H. S. (1981a). Area and contrast effects upon perceptual and imagery acuity. *Journal of Experimental Psychology: Human Perception and Performance* 7:825–832.

Finke, R. A., and Kurtzman, H. S. (1981b). Mapping the visual field in mental imagery. *Journal of Experimental Psychology: General* 110:501–517.

Finke, R. A., and Kurtzman, H. S. (1981c). Methodological considerations in experiments on imagery acuity. *Journal of Experimental Psychology: Human Perception and Performance* 7:848–854.

Finke, R. A., and Pinker, S. (1982). Spontaneous imagery scanning in mental extrapolation. *Journal of Experimental Psychology: Learning, Memory, and Cognition* 8:142–147.

Finke, R. A., and Pinker, S. (1983). Directional scanning of remembered visual patterns. *Journal of Experimental Psychology: Learning, Memory, and Cognition* 9:398–410.

Finke, R. A., Pinker, S., and Farah, M. J. (in press). Reinterpreting visual patterns in mental imagery. *Cognitive Science.*

Finke, R. A., and Schmidt, M. J. (1977). Orientation-specific color aftereffects following imagination. *Journal of Experimental Psychology: Human Perception and Performance* 3:599–606.

Finke, R. A., and Schmidt, M. J. (1978). The quantitative measure of pattern representation in images using orientation-specific color aftereffects. *Perception & Psychophysics* 23:515–520.

Finke, R. A., and Shepard, R. N. (1986). Visual functions of mental imagery. In K. R. Boff, L. Kaufman, and J. Thomas, eds., *Handbook of perception and human performance*, vol. 2. New York: Wiley-Interscience.

Finke, R. A., and Shyi, G. C.-W. (1988). Mental extrapolation and representational momentum for complex implied motions. *Journal of Experimental Psychology: Learning, Memory, and Cognition* 14:112–120.

Finke, R. A., and Slayton, K. (1988). Explorations of creative visual synthesis in mental imagery. *Memory & Cognition* 16:252–257.

Fiske, S. T., Taylor, S. E., Etcoff, N. L., and Laufer, J. K. (1979). Imaging, empathy, and causal attribution. *Journal of Experimental Social Psychology* 15:356–377.

Fodor, J. A. (1975). *The language of thought.* New York: Crowell.

Fodor, J. A. (1983). *The modularity of mind.* Cambridge, Mass.: M.I.T. Press.

Forisha, B. L. (1978). Mental imagery and creativity: Review and speculations. *Journal of Mental Imagery* 2:209–238.

Franks, J. J., and Bransford, J. D. (1971). Abstraction of visual patterns. *Journal of Experimental Psychology* 90:65–74.

Freyd, J. J. (1983a). Dynamic mental representations and apparent accelerated motion. Doctoral dissertation, Stanford University.

Freyd, J. J. (1983b). The mental representation of movement when static stimuli are viewed. *Perception & Psychophysics* 33:575–581.

Freyd, J. J. (1983c). Representing the dynamics of a static form. *Memory & Cognition* 11:342–346.

Freyd, J. J. (1987). Dynamic mental representations. *Psychological Review* 94:427–438.

Freyd, J. J., and Finke, R. A. (1984a). Facilitation of length discrimination using real and imagined context frames. *American Journal of Psychology* 97:323–341.

Freyd, J. J., and Finke, R. A. (1984b). Representational momentum. *Journal of Experimental Psychology: Learning, Memory, and Cognition* 10:126–132.

Freyd, J. J., and Finke, R. A. (1985). A velocity effect for representational momentum. *Bulletin of the Psychonomic Society* 23:443–446.

Freyd, J. J., and Johnson, J. Q. (1987). Probing the time course of representational momentum. *Journal of Experimental Psychology: Learning, Memory, and Cognition* 13:259–268.

Freyd, J. J., Pantzer, T. M., and Cheng, J. L. (in press). Representing statics as forces in equilibrium. *Journal of Experimental Psychology: General.*

Friedman, A. (1978). Memorial comparisons without the "mind's eye." *Journal of Verbal Learning and Verbal Behavior* 17:427–444.

Gazzaniga, M. S. (1970). *The bisected brain.* New York: Appleton-Century-Crofts.

Gibson, E. J. (1969). *Perceptual learning and development.* New York: Appleton-Century-Crofts.

Gibson, J. J. (1966). *The senses considered as perceptual systems.* Boston: Houghton Mifflin.

Gibson, J. J. (1979). *The ecological approach to visual perception.* Boston: Houghton Mifflin.

Glushko, R. J., and Cooper, L. A. (1978). Spatial comprehension and comparison processes in verification tasks. *Cognitive Psychology* 10:391–421.

Goldston, D. B., Hinrichs, J. V., and Richman, C. L. (1985). Subjects' expectations, individual variability, and the scanning of mental images. *Memory & Cognition* 13:365–370.

Gordon, I. E., and Hayward, S. (1973). Second-order isomorphism of internal representations of familiar faces. *Perception and Psychophysics* 14:334–336.

Gordon, R. (1949). An investigation into some of the factors that favor the formation of stereotyped images. *British Journal of Psychology* 39:156–167.

Graefe, T. M., and Watkins, M. J. (1980). Picture rehearsal: An effect of selectivity attending to pictures no longer in view. *Journal of Experimental Psychology: Human Learning and Memory* 6:156–162.

Gray, C. R., and Gummerman, K. (1975). The enigmatic eidetic image: A critical examination of methods, data, and theories. *Psychological Bulletin* 82:383–407.

Green, D. M., and Swets, J. A. (1966). *Signal detection theory and psychophysics.* New York: Wiley.

Greenwald, A. G. (1970). Sensory feedback mechanisms in performance control: With special reference to the ideo-motor mechanism. *Psychological Review* 77:73–99.

Gur, R. C., and Hilgard, E. R. (1975). Visual imagery and the discrimination of differences between altered pictures simultaneously and successively presented. *British Journal of Psychology* 66:341–345.

Haber, R. N. (1979). Twenty years of haunting eidetic imagery: Where's the ghost? *Behavioral and Brain Sciences* 2:583–629.

Halpern, A. R. (in press). Mental scanning in auditory imagery for songs. *Journal of Experimental Psychology: Learning, Memory, and Cognition.*

Harris, C. S. (1965). Perceptual adaptation in inverted, reversed, and displaced vision. *Psychological Review* 72:419–444.

Hartley, A. A. (1977). Mental measurement in the magnitude estimation of length. *Journal of Experimental Psychology: Human Perception and Performance* 3:622–628.

Hartley, A. A. (1981). Mental measurement of line length: The role of the standard. *Journal of Experimental Psychology: Human Perception and Performance* 7:309–317.

Hayes, J. R. (1973). On the function of visual imagery in elementary mathematics. In W. G. Chase, ed., *Visual information processing.* New York: Academic Press.

Hayes-Roth, F. (1979). Distinguishing theories of representation: A critique of Anderson's "Arguments concerning mental imagery." *Psychological Review* 86:376–392.

Hearne, K. H. (1981). Control your own dreams. *New Scientist* 24:783–785.

Hebb, D. O. (1968). Concerning imagery. *Psychological Review* 75:466–477.

Held, R. (1965). Plasticity in sensory-motor systems. *Scientific American* 213:84–94.

Held, R. (1970). Two modes of processing spatially distributed visual stimulation. In F. O. Schmidt, ed., *The neurosciences: Second study program.* New York: Rockefeller University Press.

Hilgard, E. R. (1965). *Hypnotic susceptibility.* New York: Harcourt, Brace, and World.

Hilgard, E. R. (1977). *Divided consciousness: Multiple controls in human thought and action.* New York: Wiley-Interscience.

Hilgard, J. R. (1970). *Personality and hypnosis: A study of imaginative involvement.* Chicago: University of Chicago Press.

Hinton, G. (1979). Some demonstrations of the effects of structural descriptions in mental imagery. *Cognitive Science* 3:231–250.

Hintzman, D. L., O'Dell, C. S., and Arndt, D. R. (1981). Orientation in cognitive maps. *Cognitive Psychology* 13:149–206.

Hochberg, J., and Gellman, L. (1977). The effect of landmark features on mental rotation times. *Memory & Cognition* 5:23–26.

Hock, H. S., and Tromley, C. L. (1978). Mental rotation and perceptual uprightness. *Perception & Psychophysics* 24:529–533.

Hoffman, D. D., and Richards, W. (1984). Parts of recognition. *Cognition* 18:65–96.

Hollins, M. (1985). Styles of mental imagery in blind adults. *Neuropsychologica* 23:561–566.

Holyoak, K. J. (1977). The form of analog size information in memory. *Cognitive Psychology* 9:31–51.

Hubel, D. H., and Wiesel, T. N. (1977). Functional architecture of macaque monkey visual cortex. *Proceedings of the Royal Society of London* 198:1–59.

Hutchinson, J. W., and Lockhead, G. R. (1977). Similarity as distance: A structural principle for semantic memory. *Journal of Experimental Psychology: Human Learning and Memory* 3:660–678.

Huttenlocher, J. (1968). Constructing spatial images: A strategy in reasoning. *Psychological Review* 4:277–299.

Huttenlocher, J., and Presson, C. (1973). Mental rotation and the perspective problem. *Cognitive Psychology* 4:277–299.

Intons-Peterson, M. J. (1981). Constructing and using unusual and common images. *Journal of Experimental Psychology: Human Learning and Memory* 7:133–144.

Intons-Peterson, M. J. (1983). Imagery paradigms: How vulnerable are they to experimenters' expectations? *Journal of Experimental Psychology: Human Perception and Performance* 9:394–412.

Intons-Peterson, M. J., and White, A. R. (1981). Experimenter naiveté and imagined judgments. *Journal of Experimental Psychology: Human Perception and Performance* 7:833–843.

Jagacinski, R. J., Johnson, W. W., and Miller, R. A. (1983). Quantifying the cognitive trajectories of extrapolated movements. *Journal of Experimental Psychology: Human Perception and Performance* 9:43–57.

Jamieson, D. G., and Petrusic, W. M. (1975). Relational judgments with remembered stimuli. *Perception & Psychophysics* 18:373–378.

Johnson, C. A., Keltner, J. L., and Balestrery, F. (1978). Effects of target size and eccentricity on visual detection and resolution. *Vision Research* 18:1217–1222.

Johnson, M. K., and Raye, C. L. (1981). Reality monitoring. *Psychological Review* 88:67–85.

Johnson, M. K., Raye, C. L., Wang, A. Y., and Taylor, T. H. (1979). Fact and fantasy: The roles of accuracy and variability in confusing imaginations with perceptual experiences. *Journal of Experimental Psychology: Human Learning and Memory* 5:229–240.

Jolicoeur, P., and Kosslyn, S. M. (1983). Coordinant systems in the long-term memory representations of three-dimensional shapes. *Cognitive Psychology* 15:301–345.

Jolicocur, P., and Kosslyn, S. M. (1985). Is time to scan visual images due to demand characteristics? *Memory & Cognition* 13:320–332.

Jolicoeur, P., Ullman, S., and Mackay, M. (1986). Curve tracing: A possible basic operation in the perception of spatial relations. *Memory & Cognition* 14:129–140.

Jones, P. D., and Holding, D. H. (1975). Extremely long-term persistence of the McCollough effect. *Journal of Experimental Psychology: Human Perception and Performance* 1:323–327.

Jonides, J., Kahn, R., and Rozin, P. (1975). Imagery instructions improve memory in blind subjects. *Bulletin of the Psychonomic Society* 5:424–426.

Just, M. A., and Carpenter, P. A. (1976). Eye fixations and cognitive processes. *Cognitive Psychology* 8:441–480.

Just, M. A., and Carpenter, P. A. (1985). Cognitive coordinate systems: Accounts of mental rotation and individual differences in spatial ability. *Psychological Review* 92:137–172.

Kaiser, M. K., Proffitt, D. R., and Anderson, K. (1985). Judgments of natural and anomalous trajectories in the presence and absence of motion. *Journal of Experimental Psychology: Learning, Memory, and Cognition* 11:795–803.

Kaufman, J. H., May, J. G., and Kunen, S. (1981). Interocular transfer of orientation-contingent color aftereffects with external and internal adaptation. *Perception & Psychophysics* 30:547–551.

Keenan, J. M. (1983). Qualifications and clarifications of images of concealed objects: A reply to Kerr and Neisser. *Journal of Experimental Psychology: Learning, Memory, and Cognition* 9: 222–230.

Keenan, J. M., and Moore, R. E. (1979). Memory for images of concealed objects: A reexamination of Neisser and Kerr. *Journal of Experimental Psychology: Human Learning and Memory* 5:374–385.

Kelly, M. H., and Freyd, J. J. (1987). Explorations of representational momentum. *Cognitive Psychology* 19:369–401.

Kerr, B., Condon, S. M., and McDonald, L. A. (1985). Cognitive spatial processing and the regulation of posture. *Journal of Experimental Psychology: Human Perception and Performance* 11:617–622.

Kerr, N. H. (1983). The role of vision in "visual imagery" experiments: Evidence from the congenitally blind. *Journal of Experimental Psychology: General* 112:265–277.

Kerr, N. H., and Neisser, U. (1983). Mental images of concealed objects: New evidence. *Journal of Experimental Psychology: Learning, Memory, and Cognition* 9:212–221.

Kerst, S. M., and Howard, J. H. (1977). Mental comparisons for ordered information on abstract and concrete dimensions. *Memory & Cognition* 5:227–234.

Kerst, S. M., and Howard, J. H. (1978). Memory psychophysics for visual area and length. *Memory & Cognition* 6:327–335.

Kieras, D. (1978). Beyond pictures and words: Alternative information-processing models for imagery effects in verbal memory. *Psychological Bulletin* 85:532–554.

Klopfer, D. S. (1985). Constructing mental representations of objects from successive views. *Journal of Experimental Psychology: Human Perception and Performance* 11:566–582.

Koffka, K. (1935). *Principles of Gestalt psychology*. New York: Harcourt Brace.

Kohler, I. (1962). Experiments with goggles. *Scientific American* 206:62–86.

Kohler, W. (1947). *Gestalt psychology*. New York: Mentor/Liveright.

Kolers, P. A. (1972). *Aspects of motion perception*. Elmsford, N.Y.: Pergamon Press.

Kolers, P. A., and Pomerantz, J. R. (1971). Figural change in apparent motion. *Journal of Experimental Psychology* 87:99–108.

Kolers, P. A., and Smythe, W. E. (1979). Images, symbols, and skills. *Canadian Journal of Psychology* 33:158–184.

Koriat, A., and Norman, J. (1984). What is rotated in mental rotation? *Journal of Experimental Psychology: Learning, Memory, and Cognition* 10:421–434.

Koriat, A., and Norman, J. (1988). Frames and images: Sequential effects in mental rotation. *Journal of Experimental Psychology: Learning, Memory, and Cognition* 14:93–111.

Kosslyn, S. M. (1973). Scanning visual images: Some structural implications. *Perception & Psychophysics* 14:90–94.

Kosslyn, S. M. (1975). Information representation in visual images. *Cognitive Psychology* 7:341–370.

Kosslyn, S. M. (1976). Can imagery be distinguished from other forms of internal representation? Evidence from studies of information retrieval times. *Memory & Cognition* 4:291–297.

Kosslyn, S. M. (1978). Measuring the visual angle of the mind's eye. *Cognitive Psychology* 10:356–389.

Kosslyn, S. M. (1980). *Image and mind*. Cambridge, Mass.: Harvard University Press.

Kosslyn, S. M. (1981). The medium and the message in mental imagery: A theory. *Psychological Review* 88:46–66.

Kosslyn, S. M. (1983). *Ghosts in the mind's machine: Creating and using images in the brain.* New York: Norton.

Kosslyn, S. M. (1987). Seeing and imagining in the cerebral hemispheres: A computational approach. *Psychological Review* 94:148–175.

Kosslyn, S. M., and Alper, S. N. (1977). On the pictorial properties of visual images: Effects of image size on memory for words. *Canadian Journal of Psychology* 31:32–40.

Kosslyn, S. M., Ball, T., and Reiser, B. J. (1978). Visual images preserve metric spatial information: Evidence from studies of image scanning. *Journal of Experimental Psychology: Human Perception and Performance* 4:47–60.

Kosslyn, S. M., Brunn, J. L., Cave, C. B., and Wallach, R. W. (1984). Individual differences in mental imagery ability: A computational analysis. *Cognition* 18:195–244.

Kosslyn, S. M., Cave, C. B., Provost, D. A., and von Gierke, S. M. (in press). Sequential processes in image generation. *Cognitive Psychology.*

Kosslyn, S. M., Holtzman, J. D., Farah, M. J., and Gazzaniga, M. S. (1985). A computational analysis of mental image generation: Evidence from functional dissociations in split-brain patients. *Journal of Experimental Psychology: General* 114:311–341.

Kosslyn, S. M., Murphy, G. L., Bemesderfer, M. E., and Feinstein, K. J. (1977). Category and continuum in mental comparisons. *Journal of Experimental Psychology: General* 106:341–375.

Kosslyn, S. M., Pick, H. L., and Fariello, G. R. (1974). Cognitive maps in children and men. *Child Development* 45:707–716.

Kosslyn, S. M., Pinker, S., Smith, G., and Shwartz, S. P. (1979). On the de-mystification of mental imagery. *Behavioral and Brain Sciences* 2:535–581.

Kosslyn, S. M., and Pomerantz, J. R. (1977). Imagery, propositions, and the form of internal representations. *Cognitive Psychology* 9:52–76.

Kosslyn, S. M., Reiser, B. J., Farah, M. J., and Fliegel, S. L. (1983). Generating visual images: Units and relations. *Journal of Experimental Psychology: General* 112:278–303.

Kosslyn, S. M., and Shwartz, S. P. (1977). A simulation of visual imagery. *Cognitive Science* 1:265–295.

Kroll, N. E. A., Parks, T., Parkinson, S. P., Bieber, S. L., and Johnson, A. L. (1970). Short-term memory while shadowing: Recall of visually and aurally presented letters. *Journal of Experimental Psychology* 85:220–224.

Kroll, N. E. A., Schepeler, E. M., and Angin, K. T. (1986). Bizarre imagery: The misremembered mnemonic. *Journal of Experimental Psychology: Learning, Memory, and Cognition* 12:42–53.

Krumhansl, C. L., and Kessler, E. J. (1982). Tracing the dynamic changes in perceived tonal organization in a spatial representation of musical keys. *Psychological Review* 89:334–368.

Kubovy, M., and Podgorny, P. (1981). Does pattern matching require the normalization of size and orientation? *Perception & Psychophysics* 30:24–28.

Kunen, S., Green, D., and Waterman, D. (1979). Spread of encoding effects within the nonverbal visual domain. *Journal of Experimental Psychology: Human Learning and Memory* 5:574–584.

Kunen, S., and May, J. G. (1980). Spatial frequency content of visual imagery. *Perception & Psychophysics* 28:555–559.

La Berge, S. P. (1980). Lucid dreaming as a learnable skill: A case study. *Perceptual and Motor Skills* 51:1039–1042.

Larsen, A., and Bundesen, C. (1978). Size scaling in visual pattern recognition. *Journal of Experimental Psychology: Human Perception and Performance* 4:1–20.

Lea, G. (1975). Chronometric analysis of the method of loci. *Journal of Experimental Psychology: Human Perception and Performance* 1:95–104.

Levine, D. N., Warach, J., and Farah, M. (1985). Two visual systems in mental imagery: Dissociation of "what" and "where" in imagery disorders due to bilateral posterior cerebral lesions. *Neurology* 35:1010–1018.

Levine, M. (1987). *Effective problem solving*. Englewood Cliffs, N.J.: Prentice-Hall.

Levine, M., Jankovic, I. N., and Palij, M. (1982). Principles of spatial problem solving. *Journal of Experimental Psychology: General* 111:157–175.

Lindauer, M. S. (1977). Imagery from the point of view of psychological aesthetics, the arts, and creativity. *Journal of Mental Imagery* 1:343–362.

Lindsay, P. H., and Norman, D. A. (1977). *Human information processing*. New York: Academic Press.

Loftus, E. F. (1979). *Eyewitness testimony*. Cambridge, Mass.: Harvard University Press.

Loftus, E. F., and Loftus, G. R. (1980). On the permanence of stored information in the human brain. *American Psychologist* 35:409–420.

Loftus, E. F., Miller, D. G., and Burns, H. J. (1978). Semantic integration of verbal information into a visual memory. *Journal of Experimental Psychology: Human Learning and Memory* 4:19–31.

Loftus, G. (1985). Johannes Kepler's computer simulation of the universe: Some remarks about theory in psychology. *Behavior Research Methods, Instruments, & Computers* 17:149–156.

Lorayne, H., and Lucas, J. (1974). *The memory book*. New York: Ballantine.

Lynch, K. (1960). *The image of the city*. Cambridge, Mass.: M.I.T. Press.

McCloskey, M., and Kohl, D. (1983). Naive physics: The curvilinear impetus principle and its role in interactions with moving objects. *Journal of Experimental Psychology: Learning, Memory, and Cognition* 9:146–156.

McCloskey, M., and Zaragoza, M. (1985). Misleading postevent information and memory for events: Arguments and evidence against memory impairment hypotheses. *Journal of Experimental Psychology: General* 114:1–16.

McCollough, C. (1965). Color adaptation of edge-detectors in the human visual system. *Science* 149:1115–1116.

McDaniel, M. A., and Einstein, G. O. (1986). Bizarre imagery as an effective memory aid: The importance of distinctiveness. *Journal of Experimental Psychology: Learning, Memory, and Cognition* 12:54–65.

McGee, M. G. (1979). *Human spatial abilities: Sources of sex differences*. New York: Praeger.

McKim, R. H. (1980). *Experiences in visual thinking*. Monterey, Calif.: Brooks/Cole.

McNamara, T. P. (1986). Mental representations of spatial relations. *Cognitive Psychology* 18:87–121.

Maffei, L., and Fiorentini, A. (1977). Spatial frequency rows in the striate visual cortex. *Vision Research* 17:257–264.

Maki, R. H. (1981). Categorization and distance effects with spatial linear orders. *Journal of Experimental Psychology: Human Learning and Memory* 7:15–32.

Malmstrom, F. B., and Randle, R. J. (1976). Effects of visual imagery on the accommodation response. *Perception & Psychophysics* 19:450–453.

Marcel, A. J. (1983). Conscious and unconscious perception: Experiments on visual masking and word recognition. *Cognitive Psychology* 15:197–237.

Marks, D. F. (1973). Visual imagery differences in the recall of pictures. *British Journal of Psychology* 64:17–24.

Marks, D. F. (1983). Mental imagery and consciousness: A theoretical review. In A. A. Sheikh, ed., *Imagery: Current theory, research and application.* New York: Wiley-Interscience.

Marmor, G. S., and Zaback, L. A. (1976). Mental rotation by the blind: Does mental rotation depend on visual imagery? *Journal of Experimental Psychology: Human Perception and Performance* 2:515–521.

Marr, D. (1982). *Vision.* San Francisco: W. H. Freeman.

Marr, D., and Nishihara, H. K. (1978). Representation and recognition of the spatial organization of three-dimensional shapes. *Proceedings of the Royal Society of London* 200:269–294.

Metzler, J., and Shepard, R. N. (1974). Transformational studies of the internal representation of three-dimensional objects. In R. L. Solso, ed., *Theories in cognitive psychology: The Loyola Symposium.* Potomac, Md.: Erlbaum.

Minsky, M., and Papert, S. (1972). *Perceptrons.* Cambridge, Mass.: M.I.T. Press.

Mitchell, D. B., and Richman, C. L. (1980). Confirmed reservations: Mental travel. *Journal of Experimental Psychology: Human Perception and Performance* 6:58–66.

Moar, I., and Bower, G. H. (1983). Inconsistency in spatial knowledge. *Memory & Cognition* 11:107–113.

Morris, P. E., and Reid, R. L. (1973). Recognition and recall: Latency and recurrence of images. *British Journal of Psychology* 64:161–167.

Moyer, R. S. (1973). Comparing objects in memory: Evidence suggesting an internal psychophysics. *Perception & Psychophysics* 13:180–184.

Moyer, R. S., and Bayer, R. H. (1976). Mental comparison and the symbolic distance effect. *Cognitive Psychology* 8:228–246.

Moyer, R. S., Bradley, D. R., Sorensen, M. H., Whiting, J. C., and Mansfield, D. P. (1978). Psychophysical functions for perceived and remembered size. *Science* 200:330–332.

Murphy, G. L., and Hutchinson, J. W. (1982). Memory for forms: Common memory formats for verbal and visual stimulus presentations. *Memory & Cognition* 10:54–61.

Nappe, G. W., and Wollen, K. A. (1973). Effects of instructions to form common and bizarre mental images on retention. *Journal of Experimental Psychology* 100:6–8.

Neisser, U. (1967). *Cognitive psychology.* Englewood Cliffs, N.J.: Prentice-Hall.

Neisser, U. (1976). *Cognition and reality.* San Francisco: W. H. Freeman.

Neisser, U., and Kerr, N. (1973). Spatial and mnemonic properties of visual images. *Cognitive Psychology* 5:138–150.

Neiworth, J. J., and Rilling, M. E. (1987). A method for studying imagery in animals. *Journal of Experimental Psychology: Animal Behavioral Processes* 13:203–214.

Newell, A., and Simon, H. (1972). *Human problem solving.* Englewood Cliffs, N.J.: Prentice-Hall.

Nickerson, R. A., and Adams, M. J. (1979). Long-term memory for a common object. *Cognitive Psychology* 11:287–307.

Nicklaus, J. (1974). *Golf my way.* New York: Simon & Schuster.

Nielsen, G. D., and Smith, E. E. (1973). Imaginal and verbal representations in short-term recognition of visual forms. *Journal of Experimental Psychology* 101:375–378.

O'Brien, E. J., and Wolford, C. R. (1982). Effects of delay in testing on retention of plausible versus bizarre mental images. *Journal of Experimental Psychology: Learning, Memory, and Cognition* 8:148–152.

Olton, D. S. (1977). Spatial memory. *Scientific American* 236:82–98.

Orne, M. T. (1962). On the social psychology of the psychology experiment: With particular reference to demand characteristics and their implications. *American Psychologist* 17:776–783.

Over, R., and Broerse, J. (1972). Imagined lines fail to induce contour masking. *Psychonomic Science* 29:203–204.

Paivio, A. (1969). Mental imagery in associative learning and memory. *Psychological Review* 76:241–263.

Paivio, A. (1975). Perceptual comparisons through the mind's eye. *Memory & Cognition* 3:635–647.

Paivio, A. (1977). Images, propositions, and knowledge. In J. M. Nicholas, ed., *Images, perception and knowledge.* Dordrecht, Holland: Reidel.

Paivio, A. (1978). Mental comparisons involving abstract attributes. *Memory & Cognition* 6:199–208.

Paivio, A. (1979). *Imagery and verbal processes.* Hillsdale, N.J.: Erlbaum.

Paivio, A., and Csapo, K. (1973). Picture superiority in free recall: Imagery or dual coding? *Cognitive Psychology* 5:176–206.

Paivio, A., and Marschark, M. (1980). Comparative judgments of animal intelligence and pleasantness. *Memory & Cognition* 8:39–48.

Palmer, S. E. (1975). The effects of contextual scenes on the identification of objects. *Memory & Cognition* 3:519–526.

Palmer, S. E. (1977). Hierarchical structure in perceptual representation. *Cognitive Psychology* 9:441–474.

Parsons, L. M. (1987a). Imagined spatial transformation of one's body. *Journal of Experimental Psychology: General* 116:172–191.

Parsons, L. M. (1987b). Imagined spatial transformation of one's hands and feet. *Cognitive Psychology* 19:178–241.

Payne, D. G. (1986). Hypermnesia for pictures and words. Testing the recall level hypothesis. *Journal of Experimental Psychology: Learning, Memory, and Cognition* 12:16–29.

Perky, C. W. (1910). An experimental study of imagination. *American Journal of Psychology* 21:442–452.

Perls, F. (1970). *Gestalt therapy verbatim.* New York: Bantam, 1970.

Peterson, M. J., and Graham, S. E. (1974). Visual detection and visual imagery. *Journal of Experimental Psychology* 103:509–514.

Pinker, S. (1980). Mental imagery and the third dimension. *Journal of Experimental Psychology: General* 109:354–371.

Pinker, S. (1984). Visual cognition: An introduction. *Cognition* 18:1–63.

Pinker, S., Choate, P., and Finke, R. A. (1984). Mental extrapolation in patterns reconstructed from memory. *Memory & Cognition* 12:207–218.

Pinker, S., and Finke, R. A. (1980). Emergent two-dimensional patterns in images rotated in depth. *Journal of Experimental Psychology: Human Perception and Performance* 6:244–264.

Pinker, S., and Kosslyn, S. M. (1978). The representation and manipulation of three-dimensional space in mental images. *Journal of Mental Imagery* 2:69–84.

Pinker, S., and Kosslyn, S. M. (1983). Theories of mental imagery. In A. A. Sheikh, ed., *Imagery: Current theory, research, and application.* New York: Wiley-Interscience.

Podgorny, P., and Shepard, R. N. (1978). Functional representations common to visual perception and imagination. *Journal of Experimental Psychology: Human Perception and Performance* 4:21–35.

Podgorny, P., and Shepard, R. N. (1983). The distribution of visual attention over space. *Journal of Experimental Psychology: Human Perception and Performance* 9:380–393.

Poggio, T. (1984). Vision by man and machine. *Scientific American* 250:106–116.

Polanyi, M. (1962). *Personal knowledge: Towards a post-critical philosophy.* Chicago: University of Chicago Press.

Polya, G. (1957). *How to solve it.* Garden City, N.Y.: Doubleday/Anchor.

Posner, M. I. (1978). *Chronometric explorations of mind.* Hillsdale, N.J.: Erlbaum.

Posner, M. I., Boies, S. J., Eichelman, W. H., and Taylor, R. L. (1969). Retention of visual and name codes of single letters. *Journal of Experimental Psychology Monograph* 79 (1, Pt. 2).

Posner, M. I., and Keele, S. W. (1968). On the genesis of abstract ideas. *Journal of Experimental Psychology* 77:353–363.

Posner, M. I., and Keele, S. W. (1970). Retention of abstract ideas. *Journal of Experimental Psychology* 83:304–308.

Potter, M. C., and Falconer, B. A. (1975). Time to understand pictures and words. *Nature* 253:437–438.

Pylyshyn, Z. W. (1973). What the mind's eye tells the mind's brain: A critique of mental imagery. *Psychological Bulletin* 80:1–24.

Pylyshyn, Z. W. (1978). Imagery and artificial intelligence. In C. W. Savage, ed., *Minnesota studies in the philosophy of science,* vol. 9. Minneapolis: University of Minnesota Press.

Pylyshyn, Z. W. (1979). The rate of "mental rotation" of images: A test of a holistic analogue hypothesis. *Memory & Cognition* 7:19–28.

Pylyshyn, Z. W. (1981). The imagery debate: Analogue media versus tacit knowledge. *Psychological Review* 88:16–45.

Pylyshyn, Z. W. (1984). *Computation and cognition: Toward a foundation for cognitive science.* Cambridge, Mass.: M.I.T. Press.

Reed, S. K. (1974). Structural descriptions and the limitations of visual images. *Memory & Cognition* 2:329–336.

Reed, S. K., Hock, H. S., and Lockhead, G. R. (1983). Tacit knowledge and the effect of pattern configuration on mental scanning. *Memory & Cognition* 11:137–143.

Reed, S. K., and Johnsen, J. A. (1975). Detection of parts in patterns and images. *Memory & Cognition* 3:569–575.

Reeves, A. (1980). Visual imagery in backward masking. *Perception & Psychophysics* 28:118–124.

Reeves, A., and Segal, S. J. (1973). Effects of visual imagery on visual sensitivity and pupil diameter. *Perceptual and Motor Skills* 36:1091–1098.

Rhodes, G., and O'Leary, A. (1985). Imagery effects on early visual processing. *Perception & Psychophysics* 37:382–388.

Richardson, A. (1967). Mental practice: A review and discussion. *Research Quarterly* 38:95–107.

Richardson, A. (1969). *Mental imagery.* New York: Springer.

Richardson, J. T. E. (1980). *Mental imagery and human memory.* New York: St. Martin's Press.

Richman, C. L., Mitchell, D. B., and Reznick, J. S. (1979). Mental travel: Some reservations. *Journal of Experimental Psychology: Human Perception and Performance* 5:13–18.

Riggs, L. A. (1965). Visual acuity. In C. H. Graham, ed., *Vision and visual perception.* New York: Wiley.

Ritchey, G. H., and Beal, C. R. (1980). Image detail and recall: Evidence for within-item elaboration. *Journal of Experimental Psychology: Human Learning and Memory* 6:66–76.

Robertson, L. C., and Palmer, S. E. (1983). Holistic processes in the perception and transformation of disoriented figures. *Journal of Experimental Psychology: Human Perception and Performance* 9:203–214.

Robertson, L. C., Palmer, S. E., and Gomez, L. M. (1987). Reference frames in mental rotation. *Journal of Experimental Psychology: Learning, Memory, and Cognition* 13:368–379.

Robins, C., and Shepard, R. N. (1977). Spatio-temporal probing of apparent rotational movement. *Perception & Psychophysics* 22:12–18.

Rock, I. (1973). *Orientation and form.* New York: Academic Press.

Rock, I. (1983). *The logic of perception.* Cambridge: Mass.: M.I.T. Press.

Rock, I., and DiVita, J. (1987). A case of viewer-centered object perception. *Cognitive Psychology* 19:280–293.

Rock, I., DiVita, J., and Barbeito, R. (1981). The effect on form perception of change in orientation in the third dimension. *Journal of Experimental Psychology: Human Perception and Performance* 7:719–732.

Rosenbaum, D. A. (1975). Perception and extrapolation of velocity and acceleration. *Journal of Experimental Psychology: Human Perception and Performance* 1:395–403.

Rosenthal, R. (1976). *Experimenter effects in behavioral research.* New York: Halsted Press.

Roth, J. D., and Kosslyn, S. M. (in press). Construction of the third dimension in mental imagery. *Cognitive Psychology.*

Sadalla, E. K., Burroughs, W. J., and Staplin, L. J. (1980). Reference points in spatial cognition. *Journal of Experimental Psychology: Human Learning and Memory* 6:516–528.

Sagi, D., and Julesz, B. (1985). "Where" and "what" in vision. *Science* 228.1217–1219.

Schiller, P. H., Finlay, B. L., and Volman, S. F. (1976). Quantitative studies of single-cell properties in monkey striate cortex: I–V. *Journal of Neurophysiology* 39:1288–1374.

Schneider, G. E. (1969). Two visual systems. *Science* 163:895–902.

Seamon, J. G. (1976). Effects of generation processes on probe identification time. *Memory & Cognition* 4:759–762.

Segal, S. J., and Fusella, V. (1970). Influences of imaged pictures and sounds on detection of visual and auditory signals. *Journal of Experimental Psychology* 83:458–464.

Sekuler, R., and Nash, D. (1972). Speed of size scaling in human vision. *Psychonomic Science* 27:93–94.

Seymour, P. (1974). Generation of a pictorial code. *Memory & Cognition* 2:224–232.

Sheehan, P. W. (1971). The role of imagery in incidental learning. *British Journal of Psychology* 62:235–243.

Sheehan, P. W. (1972). *The function and nature of imagery.* New York: Academic Press.

Sheehan, P. W., and Neisser, U. (1969). Some variables affecting the vividness of imagery in recall. *British Journal of Psychology* 60:71–80.

Sheehan, P. W., and Tilden, J. (1983). Effects of suggestibility and hypnosis on accurate and distorted retrieval from memory. *Journal of Experimental Psychology: Learning, Memory, and Cognition* 9:283–293.

Sheikh, A. A. (1983). *Imagery: Current theory, research, and application.* New York: Wiley.

Shepard, R. N. (1966). Learning and recall as organization and search. *Journal of Verbal Learning and Verbal Behavior* 5:201–204.

Shepard, R. N. (1967). Recognition memory for words, sentences, and pictures. *Journal of Verbal Learning and Verbal Behavior* 6:156–163.

Shepard, R. N. (1975). Form, formation and transformation of internal representations. In R. L. Solso, ed., *Information processing and cognition: The Loyola symposium.* Hillsdale, N.J.: Erlbaum.

Shepard, R. N. (1978a). Externalization of mental images and the act of creation. In B. S. Randhawa and W. E. Coffman, eds., *Visual learning, thinking, and communication.* New York: Academic Press.

Shepard, R. N. (1978b). The mental image. *American Psychologist* 33:125–137.

Shepard, R. N. (1980). Multidimensional scaling, tree-fitting, and clustering. *Science* 210:390–398.

Shepard, R. N. (1981). Psychophysical complementarity. In M. Kubovy and J. R. Pomerantz, eds., *Perceptual organization.* Hillsdale, N.J.: Erlbaum.

Shepard, R. N. (1982). Geometric approximations to the structure of musical pitch. *Psychological Review* 89:305–333.

Shepard, R. N. (1984). Ecological constraints on internal representation: Resonant kinematics of perceiving, imagining, thinking, and dreaming. *Psychological Review* 91:417–447.

Shepard, R. N. (1987). Evolution of a mesh between principles of the mind and regularities of the world. In J. Dupré, ed., *The latest and best essays on evolution and optimality.* Cambridge, Mass.: M.I.T. Press.

Shepard, R. N. (1988). The imagination of the scientist. In K. Egan and D. Nadaner, eds., *Imagination and education.* New York: Teachers College Press.

Shepard, R. N., and Arabie, P. (1979). Additive clustering: Representation of similarities as combinations of discrete overlapping properties. *Psychological Review* 86:87–123.

Shepard, R. N., and Cermak, G. W. (1973). Perceptual-cognitive explorations of a toroidal set of free-form stimuli. *Cognitive Psychology* 4:351–377.

Shepard, R. N., and Chipman, S. (1970). Second-order isomorphism of internal representations: Shapes of states. *Cognitive Psychology* 1:1–17.

Shepard, R. N., and Cooper, L. A. (1982). *Mental images and their transformations.* Cambridge, Mass.: M.I.T. Press.

Shepard, R. N., and Feng, C. (1972). A chronometric study of mental paper folding. *Cognitive Psychology* 3:228–243.

Shepard, R. N., and Hurwitz, S. (1984). Upward direction, mental rotation, and discrimination of left and right turns in maps. *Cognition* 18:161–193.

Shepard, R. N., and Judd, S. A. (1976). Perceptual illusion of rotation of three-dimensional objects. *Science* 191:952–954.

Shepard, R. N., Kilpatric, D. W., and Cunningham, J. P. (1975). The internal representation of numbers. *Cognitive Psychology* 7:82–138.

Shepard, R. N., and Metzler, J. (1971). Mental rotation of three-dimensional objects. *Science* 171:701–703.

Shepard, R. N., and Podgorny, P. (1978). Cognitive processes that resemble perceptual processes. In W. K. Estes, ed., *Handbook of learning and cognitive processes,* vol. 5. Hillsdale, N.J.: Erlbaum.

Shepard, R. N., and Zare, S. (1983). Path-guided apparent motion. *Science* 220:632–634.

Shepard, S., and Metzler, D. (1988). Mental rotation: Effects of stimulus dimensionality and type of task. *Journal of Experimental Psychology: Human Perception and Performance* 14:3–11.

Simon, H. A., and Barenfeld, M. (1969). Information processing analysis of perceptual processes in problem solving. *Psychological Review* 76:473–483.

Singer, G., and Sheehan, P. W. (1965). The effect of demand characteristics on the figural after-effect with real and imaged inducing figures. *American Journal of Psychology* 78:96–101.

Singer, J. L. (1974). *Imagery and daydream methods in psychotherapy and behavior modification.* New York: Academic Press, 1974.

Skowbo, D., Timney, B. N., Gentry, T. A., and Morant, R. B. (1975). McCollough effects: Experimental findings and theoretical accounts. *Psychological Bulletin* 82:497–510.

Slee, J. A. (1980). Individual differences in visual imagery ability and the retrieval of visual appearances. *Journal of Mental Imagery* 4:93–113.

Spanos, N. P., and McPeake, J. D. (1975). Involvement in everyday imaginative activities, attitudes toward hypnosis, and hypnotic susceptibility. *Journal of Personality and Social Psychology* 31:594–598.

Sperling, G. (1960). The information available in brief visual presentations. *Psychological Monographs* 74:1–29.

Springer, S. P., and Deutsch, G. (1981). *Left brain, right brain.* San Francisco: Freeman.

Standing, L. (1973). Learning 10,000 pictures. *Quarterly Journal of Experimental Psychology* 25:207–222.

Sternberg, R. J. (1977). *Intelligence information processing and analogical reasoning: The componential analysis of human abilities.* Hillsdale, N.J.: Erlbaum.

Stevens, A., and Coupe, P. (1978). Distortions in judged spatial relations. *Cognitive Psychology* 10:422–437.

Stevens, S. S. (1975). *Psychophysics: Introduction to its perceptual, neural, and social prospects.* New York: Wiley.

Suinn, R. M. (1980). *Psychology in sports: Methods and applications.* Minneapolis: Burgess.

Tellegen, A., and Atkinson, G. (1974). Openness to absorbing and self-altering experiences ("absorption"), a trait related to hypnotic susceptibility. *Journal of Abnormal Psychology* 83:268–277.

Teuber, H.-L. (1978). The brain and human behavior. In R. Held, H. W. Liebowitz, and H.-L. Teuber, eds., *Handbook of sensory physiology: Perception.* Berlin: Springer-Verlag.

Thompson, A. L., and Klatzky, R. L. (1978). Studies of visual synthesis: Integration of fragments into forms. *Journal of Experimental Psychology: Human Perception and Performance* 4:244–263.

Thomson, J. A. (1983). Is continuous visual monitoring necessary in visually guided locomotion? *Journal of Experimental Psychology: Human Perception and Performance* 9:427–443.

Thorndyke, P. W. (1981). Distance estimation from cognitive maps. *Cognitive Psychology* 13:526–550.

Tolman, E. C. (1948). Cognitive maps in rats and men. *Psychological Review* 55:189–208.

Tulving, E., and Thomson, D. M. (1973). Encoding specificity and retrieval processes in episodic memory. *Psychological Review* 80:352–373.

Tversky, A. (1977). Features of similarity. *Psychological Review* 84:327–352.

Tversky, B. (1975). Pictorial encoding of sentences in sentence-picture comparison. *Quarterly Journal of Experimental Psychology* 27:405–410.

Tversky, B. (1981). Distortions in memory for maps. *Cognitive Psychology* 13:407–433.

Ullman, S. (1984). Visual routines. *Cognition* 18:97–160.

Wallace, B. (1984). Apparent equivalence between perception and imagery in the production of various visual illusions. *Memory & Cognition* 12:156–162.

Weber, R. J., and Castleman, J. (1970). The time it takes to imagine. *Perception & Psychophysics* 8:165–168.

Weber, R. J., and Malmstrom, F. V. (1979). Measuring the size of mental images. *Journal of Experimental Psychology: Human Perception and Performance* 5:1–12.

Welch, R. B. (1978). *Perceptual modification: Adapting to altered sensory environments.* New York: Academic Press.

White, K., Sheehan, P. W., and Ashton, R. (1977). Imagery assessment: A survey of self-report measures. *Journal of Mental Imagery* 1:145–170.

Wickelgren, W. A. (1974). *How to solve problems.* San Francisco: Freeman.

Wilton, R. N. (1979). Knowledge of spatial relations: The specification of the information used in making inferences. *Quarterly Journal of Experimental Psychology* 31:133–146.

Wollen, K. A., Weber, A., and Lowry, D. H. (1972). Bizarreness versus interaction of mental images as determinants of learning. *Cognitive Psychology* 3:518–523.

Wolpe, J. (1969). *The practice of behavioral therapy.* New York: Pergamon, 1969.

Yates, F. A. (1966). *The art of memory.* Chicago: University of Chicago Press.

Yuille, J. C., and Steiger, J. H. (1982). Nonholistic processing in mental rotation: Some suggestive evidence. *Perception & Psychophysics* 31:201–209.

Zimler, J., and Keenan, J. M. (1983). Imagery in the congenitally blind: How visual are visual images? *Journal of Experimental Psychology: Learning, Memory, and Cognition* 9:269–282.

Index

Absorption, 139
Accommodation, visual, 56
Acuity, visual. *See* Visual acuity
Adaptation, visual. *See* Visual
  adaptation
Agnosia, visual, 149
Ambiguous figures, 126, 128–129, 133–
  134, 138, 146. *See also* Visual illusions
Anderson, John R., 21, 24–25, 64, 95,
  142–143, 147, 157
Apparent motion, visual, 114
Art, visual, 154
Attention, selective, 35, 51, 100
Auditory perception, 55

Beethoven, Ludwig van, 154
Bower, Gordon H., 10–11, 21, 56, 84,
  134, 142, 157–158, 168
Brain damage, 147–150
Brooks, Lee R., 3–5, 8, 19, 55, 158

Cognitive maps. *See also* Memory, spatial; Memory, distortions of
  boundary effects in, 81–84
  distortions of, 80–84, 85–86
  inconsistencies in, 84
  landmark effects in, 81
  use in spatial navigation, 78–80, 87, 104
Cognitive penetration, 69
Color vision, 44–47
Computational models. *See* Mental imagery, computational models of
Computer simulation, 142–145. *See also*
  Formal models
Cooper, Lynn A., 51, 90–97, 100, 102,
  105, 113–114, 121–124, 130, 138, 159,
  162, 172
Creativity, 134–136, 138–140. *See also*

Dreams; Mental synthesis, creative;
  Mental images, control of

Demand characteristics, 38, 44, 49, 71–
  72, 75–77, 102, 107, 110, 115, 138, 148,
  155. *See also* Experimenter bias; Guessing, controls for
Depth of processing, 11
Descriptions. *See* Verbal processes
Detection
  auditory, 55
  visual, 42, 51, 55–57
Discrimination, visual, 52–53, 94–95
Dreams
  control of, 139–140
  function of, 139
  lucid, 139–140
Dual coding, 8–9, 21, 28. *See also* Verbal
  processes

Eidetic images, 27–28. *See also* Memory,
  photographic
Encoding specificity, 11
Euclidian surface, 62
Expectancy, effects of, 52, 72, 74–75, 97,
  132. *See also* Guessing, controls for;
  Perceptual anticipations; Response
  bias
Experimenter bias, 38–40, 42, 49, 54–55,
  71–72, 102, 110, 136, 148, 155. *See also*
  Demand characteristics
Eye movements, controls for, 32–33, 46,
  49, 54–57, 68, 75–76, 87, 101–102, 110,
  114, 155
Eyewitness testimony, 16, 154. *See also*
  Memory, distortions of

/153.32F449P>C1/

A